UNLOCK

READING & WRITING SKILLS

1

Sabina Ostrowska

CAMBRIDGE
UNIVERSITY PRESS

CAMBRIDGE
UNIVERSITY PRESS

University Printing House, Cambridge CB2 8BS, United Kingdom

Cambridge University Press is part of the University of Cambridge.

It furthers the University's mission by disseminating knowledge in the pursuit of education, learning and research at the highest international levels of excellence.

www.cambridge.org
Information on this title: www.cambridge.org/9781107613997

© Cambridge University Press 2014

First published 2014
6th printing 2015

Printed in Dubai by Oriental Press

A catalogue record for this publication is available from the British Library

ISBN 978-1-107-61399-7 Reading and Writing 1 Student's Book with Online Workbook
ISBN 978-1-107-61401-7 Reading and Writing 1 Teacher's Book with DVD
ISBN 978-1-107-67810-1 Listening and Speaking 1 Student's Book with Online Workbook
ISBN 978-1-107-66211-7 Listening and Speaking 1 Teacher's Book with DVD

Additional resources for this publication at www.cambridge.org/unlock

CONTENTS

MAP OF THE BOOK

UNIT	VIDEO	READING	VOCABULARY	
1 PEOPLE Reading 1: Friendfile (Communication studies) Reading 2: A very tall man! (Anthropology)	People	*Key reading skill*: Previewing Understanding key vocabulary Skimming Scanning to find information	Family vocabulary (e.g. *grandfather, grandmother, father, mother*)	
2 SEASONS Reading 1: The coldest city in the world (Geography) Reading 2: Cuba weather (Meteorology)	Extreme weather	*Key reading skill*: Scanning to find information Previewing Understanding key vocabulary	Adjectives to describe the weather (e.g. *warm, hot, cold, sunny*)	
3 LIFESTYLE Reading 1: Can you imagine your life with no mobile phones or TV? (Anthropology) Reading 2: Timetable (Management)	Life underground	*Key reading skill*: Scanning to find information Previewing Understanding key vocabulary	Vocabulary for study (e.g. *Maths, History, Chemistry, Business*)	
4 PLACES Reading 1: A world history of maps (History) Reading 2: The Maldives: an overview (Geography)	France	*Key reading skill*: Reading for main ideas Understanding key vocabulary Previewing Scanning to find information Reading for detail	Vocabulary for places in a city (e.g. *museum, library, factory, monument*) Vocabulary for places in a country (e.g. *hill, farm, field, forest*)	
5 SPORT Reading 1: The world's top five favourite sports (Sports studies) Reading 2: Sport in Brazil (Cultural studies)	Tai-Chi and Shaolin Kung-Fu	*Key reading skill*: Using your knowledge to predict content Understanding key vocabulary Reading for main ideas Scanning to find information Scanning to predict content Reading for detail	Adjectives to describe sports (e.g. *hard, exciting, expensive, difficult*)	
6 JOBS Reading 1: Find_my_job.com (Business and management) Reading 2: Job emails (Business and management)	Dabbawallas	*Key reading skill*: Reading for detail Previewing Understanding key vocabulary Scanning to find information Working out meaning from context	Vocabulary for jobs (e.g. *vet, fireman, manages people, prepares food*)	

GRAMMAR	CRITICAL THINKING	WRITING
Nouns and verbs Singular and plural nouns **Grammar for writing**: • The verb *be* • Personal pronouns • Possessive determiners	• Analyze a family tree • Draw a family tree	**Academic writing skills**: • Punctuation **Writing task type**: Write descriptive sentences. **Writing task**: Write about somebody in your family.
Adjectives and nouns Noun phrases **Grammar for writing**: • Subject and verb • Prepositions • Prepositional phrases	• Understand a table	**Academic writing skills**: • Punctuation: capital letters **Writing task type**: Write facts. **Writing task**: Write facts about the weather in your city.
Collocations **Grammar for writing**: • Subject – verb – object • Present simple • Time expressions	• Answer personal questions about routine • Create a timetable	**Academic writing skills**: • Spelling third person singular forms **Writing task type**: Write facts. **Writing task**: Write facts about the lifestyle of a student in your class.
Noun phrases with *of* **Grammar for writing**: • *there is / there are* • Determiners: articles	• Order writing by topic • Classify words • Think of key words	**Academic writing skills**: • Spelling and punctuation: capital letters **Writing task type**: Write facts. **Writing task**: Write facts about your country.
Sports collocations Prepositions Adjectives **Grammar for writing**: • Subject – verb – adjective • Subject – verb – adverb	• Create a ideas map	**Academic writing skills**: • Commas **Writing task type**: Write facts. **Writing task**: Write facts about a popular sport in your country.
Adjective phrases **Grammar for writing**: • *must* and *have to* • Joining sentences with *and*	• Complete a questionnaire • Choose a job based on Questionnaire results	**Academic writing skills**: • Contractions **Writing task type**: Write sentences. **Writing task**: Write a description of a job for a friend.

UNIT	VIDEO	READING	VOCABULARY	
7 HOMES AND BUILDINGS Reading 1: *Architect's world expert interview* (Architecture) Reading 2: Skyscrapers (Architecture)	Building the new Shanghai	*Key reading skill*: Using visuals to predict content Understanding key vocabulary Scanning to find information Reading for detail Previewing Understanding discourse	Vocabulary for buildings (e.g. *cinema, library, hotel, train station*) Vocabulary for parts of buildings (e.g. *car park, stairs, exit, garden*) Adjectives to describe buildings (e.g. *big, modern, old, ugly*)	
8 FOOD AND CULTURE Reading 1: Tea: A world history (History) Reading 2: Ten of the best by cuisine (Hospitality management)	Mexican food	*Key reading skill*: Skimming Previewing Understanding key vocabulary Scanning to find information Reading for detail	Vocabulary for food and drink (e.g. *potatoes, coconut, yoghurt, water*)	
9 THE ANIMAL KINGDOM Reading 1: Variety in the animal kingdom (Zoology) Reading 2: The world's fastest hunters (Zoology)	South African wildlife	*Key reading skill*: Reading for main ideas Previewing Understanding key vocabulary Reading for detail Using your knowledge Skimming Scanning to find information Understanding discourse	Vocabulary to describe facts about animals (e.g. *long, high, weighs, habitat*) Vocabulary for animals (e.g. *harmless, endangered, deadliest, nocturnal*)	
10 TRANSPORT Reading 1: Transport survey (Transport and logistics) Reading 2: Transport in Bangkok: report (Urban planning)	Tokyo transport	*Key reading skill*: Working out meaning from context Previewing Using your knowledge Skimming Scanning to find information Understanding key vocabulary Reading for detail Understanding discourse	Transport collocations (e.g. *take the bus, travel by car*)	

GRAMMAR	CRITICAL THINKING	WRITING
Grammar for writing: • Comparing quantities • Comparative adjectives • Joining sentences with *but*	• Compare data	*Academic writing skills*: • Spelling: double consonants *Writing task type*: Write a comparison. *Writing task*: Write a comparison of two buildings.
Countable and uncountable nouns *Grammar for writing*: • Subject–verb agreement • Determiners: *a*, *an* and *some*	• Brainstorm • Analyze notes • Make notes	*Academic writing skills*: • Spelling *Writing task type*: Write descriptive sentences. *Writing task*: Write about food in your country for a student website.
can and *cannot* *Grammar for writing*: • Superlative adjectives	• Analyze a table of facts	*Academic writing skills*: • Spelling *Writing task type*: Write a descriptive paragraph. *Writing task*: Write a paragraph about an animal.
Quantifiers *Grammar for writing*: • Subject – verb – object • Linking sentences with pronouns	• Collect data with a survey	*Academic writing skills*: • Error correction *Writing task type*: Write a paragraph. *Writing task*: Write a paragraph about transport in your city.

UNL⌀CK UNIT STRUCTURE

The units in *Unlock Reading & Writing Skills* are carefully scaffolded so that students are taken step-by-step through the writing process.

UNLOCK YOUR KNOWLEDGE	Encourages discussion around the theme of the unit with inspiration from interesting questions and striking visuals.
WATCH AND LISTEN	Features an engaging and motivating *Discovery Education*™ video which generates interest in the topic.
READING 1	Practises the reading skills required to understand academic texts as well as the vocabulary needed to comprehend the text itself.
READING 2	Presents a second text which provides a different angle on the topic in a different genre. It is a model text for the writing task.
LANGUAGE DEVELOPMENT	Practises the vocabulary and grammar from the Readings in preparation for the writing task.
CRITICAL THINKING	Contains brainstorming, evaluative and analytical tasks as preparation for the writing task.
GRAMMAR FOR WRITING	Presents and practises grammatical structures and features needed for the writing task.
ACADEMIC WRITING SKILLS	Practises all the writing skills needed for the writing task.
WRITING TASK	Uses the skills and language learnt over the course of the unit to draft and edit the writing task. Requires students to produce a piece of academic writing. Checklists help learners to edit their work.
OBJECTIVES REVIEW	Allows students to assess how well they have mastered the skills covered in the unit.
WORDLIST	Includes the key vocabulary from the unit.

This is the unit's main learning objective. It gives learners the opportunity to use all the language and skills they have learnt in the unit.

UNL😮CK MOTIVATION

UNL😮CK YOUR KNOWLEDGE • • • • • • • • • • • •

Read the sentences (1–5) below and write the jobs from the box in the gaps. Use a dictionary to help you.

> architect   manager   software engineer
> nurse   primary school teacher

1 A _____ manages people.
2 An _____ designs buildings.
3 A _____ looks after people in
   a hospital.
4 A _____ manages software.
5 A _____ teaches young children.

PERSONALIZE

Unlock encourages students to bring their own knowledge, experiences and opinions to the topics. This motivates students to relate the topics to their own contexts.

DISCOVERY EDUCATION™ VIDEO

Thought-provoking videos from *Discovery Education*™ are included in every unit throughout the course to introduce topics, promote discussion and motivate learners. The videos provide a new angle on a wide range of academic subjects.

> " The video was excellent! It helped with raising students' interest in the topic. It was well-structured and the language level was appropriate.
>
> Maria Agata Szczerbik,
> United Arab Emirates University,
> Al-Ain, UAE "

UNLOCK CRITICAL THINKING

> *The Critical thinking sections present a difficult area in an engaging and accessible way.*
>
> Shirley Norton, London School of English, UK

BLOOM'S TAXONOMY

CREATE — create, invent, plan, compose, construct, design, imagine

decide, rate, choose, recommend, justify, assess, prioritize — **EVALUATE**

ANALYZE — explain, contrast, examine, identify, investigate, categorize

show, complete, use, classify, examine, illustrate, solve — **APPLY**

UNDERSTAND — compare, discuss, restate, predict, translate, outline

name, describe, relate, find, list, write, tell — **REMEMBER**

BLOOM'S TAXONOMY

The Critical Thinking sections in *Unlock* are based on Benjamin Bloom's classification of learning objectives. This ensures learners develop their **lower-** and **higher-order thinking skills**, ranging from demonstrating **knowledge** and **understanding** to in-depth **evaluation**.

The margin headings in the Critical Thinking sections highlight the exercises which develop Bloom's concepts.

LEARN TO THINK

Learners engage in **evaluative** and **analytical tasks** that are designed to ensure they do all of the thinking and information-gathering required for the end-of-unit writing task.

CRITICAL THINKING

UNDERSTAND

At the end of this unit, you will write facts. Look at this unit's writing task in the box below.

> Write facts about the weather in your city.

Understand a table

EXPLANATION

A *table* shows facts and numbers. It is easy to see facts and numbers in a table.

Decimal numbers have a full stop in them – for example, 1.1, 1.7, 2.7. When we say decimal numbers, we use the word *point*.

1.1 one point one   1.7 one point seven   2.7 two point seven

Table 3.4: Average temperatures and rainfall in Ulaanbaatar, Mongolia

month	average temperatures (°C)	average rainfall (mm)
January	−22	1.1
February	−16	1.7
March	−7	2.7
April	+2	8.3
May	+10	13

UNL⊘CK RESEARCH

THE WORDS YOU NEED

Language Development sections provide vocabulary and grammar building tasks that are further practised in the **UNL⊘CK ONLINE** Workbook.
The glossary and end-of-unit wordlists provide definitions, pronunciation and handy summaries of all the key vocabulary.

THE CAMBRIDGE LEARNER CORPUS ⊘

The **Cambridge Learner Corpus** is a bank of official Cambridge English exam papers. Our exclusive access means we can use the corpus to carry out unique research and identify the most common errors learners make. That information is used to ensure the *Unlock* syllabus teaches the most **relevant language**.

⊘ LANGUAGE DEVELOPMENT

EXPLANATION

Nouns and verbs

Words for people, places or things are *nouns*. Words for states or actions are *verbs*. Sentences have nouns and verbs.

nouns: Tom is a **doctor**. He lives in **New York**. He works in a **hospital**.
verbs: Tom **is** a doctor. He **lives** in New York. He **works** in a hospital.

1 Read the sentences (1–7) and write the bold words in the correct places in the table below.

GRAMMAR FOR WRITING

EXPLANATION

The verb *be*

The verb *be* has three forms in the Present simple tense: *am, is, are*. After *I*, we use *am*. After *you, we* or *they*, we use *are*. After *he, she* or *it*, we use *is*.

I **am** a student.
You **are** a student. We **are** students. They **are** students.
Junko **is** a student. She **is** a student. My sister **is** a student.
Amir **is** a boxer. Sultan **is** a farmer. My grandfather **is** a doctor.
London **is** a big city. It **is** a big farm. His name **is** Tom.
Marika and Rolando **are** Italian. They **are** Italian.

1 Read the texts (A and B) and write *am, is* or *are* in the gaps.

ACADEMIC LANGUAGE

Unique research using the **Cambridge English Corpus** has been carried out into academic language, in order to provide learners with relevant, academic vocabulary from the start (CEFR A1 and above). This addresses a gap in current academic vocabulary mapping and ensures learners are presented with carefully selected words they will find essential during their studies.

GRAMMAR FOR WRITING

The grammar syllabus is carefully designed to help learners become good writers of English. There is a strong focus on sentence structure, word agreement and referencing, which are important for **coherent** and **organized** academic writing.

The language development is clear and the strong lexical focus is positive as learners feel they make more progress when they learn more vocabulary.

Colleen Wackrow,
Princess Nourah Bint Abdulrahman University, Al-Riyadh, Kingdom of Saudi Arabia

UNL🔒CK SOLUTIONS

FLEXIBLE

Unlock is available in a range of print and digital components, so teachers can mix and match according to their requirements.

UNL🔒CK ONLINE WORKBOOKS

The **UNL🔒CK ONLINE** Workbooks are accessed via activation codes packaged with the Student's Books. These **easy-to-use** workbooks provide interactive exercises, games, tasks, and further practice of the language and skills from the Student's Books in the Cambridge LMS, an engaging and modern learning environment.

CAMBRIDGE LEARNING MANAGEMENT SYSTEM (LMS)

The Cambridge LMS provides teachers with the ability to track learner progress and save valuable time thanks to automated marking functionality. Blogs, forums and other tools are also available to facilitate communication between students and teachers.

UNL🔒CK EBOOKS

The *Unlock* Student's Books and Teacher's Books are also available as interactive eBooks. With answers and *Discovery Education™* videos embedded, the eBooks provide a great alternative to the printed materials.

COURSE COMPONENTS

- Each level of *Unlock* consists of two Student's Books: **Reading & Writing** and **Listening & Speaking** and an accompanying Teacher's Book for each. Online Workbooks are packaged with each Student's Book.
- Look out for the ⬭ **UNL🔒CK ONLINE** symbols in the Student's Books which indicate that additional practice of that skill or language area is available in the Online Workbook.
- Every *Unlock* Student's Book is delivered both in print format and as an interactive **eBook for tablet devices**.
- The *Unlock* Teacher's Books contain additional writing tasks, tests, teaching tips and research projects for students.
- *Presentation Plus* **software for interactive whiteboards** is available for all Student's Books.

READING AND WRITING

Student's Book and Online Workbook Pack*	978-1-107-61399-7	978-1-107-61400-0	978-1-107-61526-7	978-1-107-61525-0
Teacher's Book with DVD*	978-1-107-61401-7	978-1-107-61403-1	978-1-107-61404-8	978-1-107-61409-3
Presentation Plus (interactive whiteboard software)	978-1-107-63800-6	978-1-107-65605-5	978-1-107-67624-4	978-1-107-68245-0

*eBook available from **www.cambridge.org/unlock**

LISTENING AND SPEAKING

Student's Book and Online Workbook Pack*	978-1-107-67810-1	978-1-107-68232-0	978-1-107-68728-8	978-1-107-63461-9
Teacher's Book with DVD*	978-1-107-66211-7	978-1-107-64280-5	978-1-107-68154-5	978-1-107-65052-7
Presentation Plus (interactive whiteboard software)	978-1-107-66424-1	978-1-107-69582-5	978-1-107-63543-2	978-1-107-64381-9

*eBook available from **www.cambridge.org/unlock**

The complete course audio is available from
www.cambridge.org/unlock

LEARNING OBJECTIVES

Watch and listen	Watch and understand a video about people and their jobs
Reading skills	Preview a text
Academic writing skills	Use capital letters and full stops in sentences
Writing task	Write descriptive sentences

PEOPLE | UNIT 1

PREPARING TO WATCH

1 Match the places (1–6) to the correct countries (a–f).

1	New Delhi	a	Italy	_____
2	New York	b	South Africa	_____
3	The Cape Peninsula	c	United States	_____
4	Cairo	d	Mexico	_____
5	Milan	e	India	_____
6	Mexico City	f	Egypt	_____

WHILE WATCHING

2 You are going to watch a video about people around the world. Watch and complete the table with the information you hear.

name	job	place
Amarel		New York, United States
Sebastian	He is an artist.	
Angela		Milan, Italy
Yasmine	She works for a magazine.	
David		The Cape Peninsula, South Africa
Geeta	She plans weddings.	

3 ▶ Watch the video again. Complete the sentences below with the correct adjectives from the box.

> beautiful   different   interesting   famous

1 The people in the video do _____ jobs.
2 Sebastian is a _____ Mexican artist.
3 Angela makes _____ clothes.
4 The people in the video all have _____ lives.

DISCUSSION

4 Work with a partner. Ask and answer the questions below.

1 Which person in the video has the most interesting job?
2 What job would you like to do in the future?
3 Where would you like to live in the future?

READING 1

PREPARING TO READ

1 Look at the text. Circle the correct answers to the questions below.

1 What is the text about?

a a sport **b** a young man **c** a family

2 Where is the text from?

a a book **b** a magazine **c** a web page

2 Read the sentences (1–4) below and write the words from the box in the gaps.

> languages   city   birth   country

1 London is a very big _____ .
2 I speak three _____ : Turkish, Arabic and English.
3 Morocco is a _____ in North Africa.
4 My date of _____ is 7 July 1993.

WHILE READING

3 Read the text and write the words from the box in the gaps (1–4).

> My hobbies and interests   My address   My life   My family

4 Read the text again. Circle the correct words to make true sentences.

1 Amir is from *Pakistan / the United Kingdom.*
2 Amir's brother is a *boxer / racing car driver.*
3 Amir's hobbies are *gaming and swimming / swimming and football.*
4 Muhammad Ali is Amir's favourite *sportsman / teacher.*
5 Falak is Amir's *sister / mother.*
6 Shah is Amir's *brother / father.*
7 Amir's address is *info@amirsfans.co.uk / amirsfans@info.co.uk*
8 His favourite football team is *Manchester City / Bolton Wanderers.*

5 Read the summary below and circle the correct words.

> Amir Khan is a (1) *boxer / teacher.* He is from (2) *Bolton / Manchester*
> in the United Kingdom. His date of birth is 8 December
> (3) *1986 / 1996.* His brother's name is (4) *Haroon / Shah.*
> His father is (5) *Muhammad Ali / Shah Khan.*

DISCUSSION

6 Work with a partner. Ask and answer the questions (1–6) below.

1 What is your name?
2 Where are you from?
3 What is your date of birth?
4 What are your brothers' and sisters' names?
5 What languages do you speak?
6 How tall are you?

FriendFile

MY PROFILE
Amir Khan

My personal information

First name: Amir
Last name: Khan
Date of birth: 8 December 1986
City: Bolton
Country: United Kingdom
Languages: English, Urdu, Punjabi
Job: Boxer

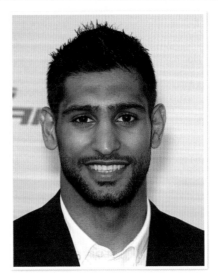

1

Email: info@amirsfans.co.uk

2

Mother: Falak
Father: Shah
Brother: Haroon

3

Hobbies: swimming, football
Favourite football club:
Bolton Wanderers
Favourite sportsman:
Muhammad Ali

4

I'm Amir Khan. My mother and father are from Pakistan. I speak three languages: English, Urdu and Punjabi. I am a boxer. I have won many boxing matches. My brother's name is Haroon. He is a boxer too. I like reading, swimming and watching football.

PREPARING TO READ

1 Look at the text. Circle the correct options (a–c).

1 The photo is of
   a a typical man.   **b** an unusual man.   **c** an English man.

2 The text is about
   a a racing car driver.   **b** a boxer.   **c** a very tall man.

3 The text is from
   a a book.   **b** a magazine.   **c** a web page.

Previewing

Previewing means looking at a text before you read it. When we preview a text, we look at the text and think about the questions below.

- Are there photographs?
- What is in the photographs?
- What is the title of the text?
- Where is the text from? (a book? a magazine? a web page?)

2 Check the meaning of the bold words in the sentences (1–6) below. Use the glossary on page 194 to help you.

1 My sister is 188 cm. She is very **tall**!
2 My brother is a student. He **lives** in London.
3 My father is a teacher. He **works** in a school.
4 Meltem loves **clothes** and **shoes**.
5 Chaiwat's **height** is 169 cm.
6 Khalid's father is a **farmer**.

A VERY tall man!

Sultan Kösen is from Turkey. He lives in Mardin in Turkey. He lives with his family. Sultan lives with his mother, his three brothers and his sister.

Sultan is a typical farmer. His hobby is watching TV. He is interested in music. His height is unusual. He is 251 cm tall – that is *very* tall. Sultan is the tallest man in the world. His mother, brothers and sister are normal height.

Sultan works on the farm. He has a tractor. His life is not easy. People look at him in the street. Normal clothes and shoes are too small. His clothes and shoes are very big.

Sultan speaks Turkish and English. He went to London, Paris and Madrid in Europe in 2010. He went to New York, Chicago and Los Angeles in America in 2011.

Sultan Kösen is from Turkey

WHILE READING

3 Read the text and circle the correct words in the profile below.

> ## UNUSUAL PEOPLE – PROFILE
>
> First name: (1) *Sultan / Kösen*
> Last name: (2) *Sultan / Kösen*
> Country: (3) *Turkey / America*
> City: (4) *Mardin / New York*
> Date of birth: (5) *1982 / 2011*
> Family: (6) *3 sisters and 1 brother / 1 sister and 3 brothers*
> Height: (7) *210 cm / 251 cm*

4 Read the text again. Write the correct words from the text in the gaps.

1 Sultan Kösen _____ from Turkey.
2 He _____ in Mardin in Turkey.
3 He lives with his _____ .
4 Sultan _____ a typical farmer.
5 His hobby _____ watching TV.
6 Sultan _____ Turkish and English.

DISCUSSION

5 Work with a partner. Ask and answer the questions (1–3) below.

1 Where do you live?

_____

2 Is it a nice place to live? Why? / Why not?

_____

3 Who do you live with?

_____

UNLOCK READING AND WRITING SKILLS 1

◉ LANGUAGE DEVELOPMENT

Nouns and verbs

Words for people, places or things are *nouns*. Words for states or actions are *verbs*. Sentences have nouns and verbs.

> nouns: Tom *is* a **doctor**. He lives in **New York**. He works in a **hospital**.
> verbs: Tom **is** a doctor. He **lives** in New York. He **works** in a hospital.

1 Read the sentences (1–7) and write the bold words in the correct places in the table below.

1 Marika Diana is from **Italy**.
2 Sultan Kösen **lives** on a farm.
3 My **brother** is a student.
4 Faisal's mother **works** in London.
5 London **is** a big city.
6 Amir Khan is a **boxer**.
7 Sultan's **clothes** and **shoes** are very big.

nouns	verbs

Singular and plural nouns

Nouns are *singular* or *plural*. Singular means *one*. Plural means *more than one*. We use *-s* at the end of plural nouns.

> singular nouns: Ray has a **brother**. His **brother** is a boxer.
> plural nouns: Engin has two **brothers**. His **brothers** are boxers.

2 Read the sentences (1–5) and circle the correct words.

1 My mother has four *sister / sisters*.
2 I have only one *pen / pens*.
3 My father has a *car / cars*.
4 We have two *house / houses*.
5 They have five *cat / cats*.

3 Read the sentences (1–6) and write the words from the box in the gaps.

teachers   lives   speaks   Rome   brothers   is

1 Hamdan _____ from Dubai.
2 Eriko and Tomoko are _____ . They work in a big
   school.
3 She _____ two languages: Arabic and English.
4 I live with my sister and my three _____ .
5 My grandfather _____ in Istanbul.
6 Marika Diana lives in _____ .

FAMILY VOCABULARY

4 Write the words from the box in the correct places in the table below.

grandfather   uncle   brother   mother   daughter

male	female
(1)_____	grandmother
father	(2)_____
son	(3)_____
(4)_____	sister
(5)_____	aunt

CRITICAL THINKING

At the end of this unit, you will write descriptive sentences. Look at this
unit's writing task in the box below.

Write about somebody in your family.

A family tree

A *family tree* shows the relationships in a family.

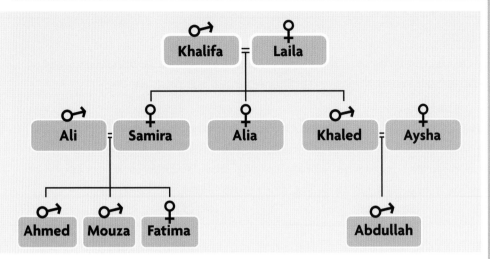

1 Work with a partner. Ask and answer the questions (1–8) about the family tree.

UNDERSTAND

1 Who is Samira's brother?
2 Who is Fatima's mother?
3 Who is Ahmed's grandmother?
4 Who are Abdullah's aunts?
5 Who are Khalifa's daughters?
6 Who is Aysha's son?
7 Who is Mouza's grandfather?
8 Who are Khaled's sisters?

2 Draw your family tree.

CREATE

3 Work with a partner. Ask and answer questions like the questions in Exercise 1 about your family trees.

WRITING

GRAMMAR FOR WRITING

The verb *be*

The verb *be* has three forms in the Present simple tense: *am, is, are*. After *I*, we use *am*. After *you, we* or *they*, we use *are*. After *he, she* or *it*, we use *is*.

I **am** a student.
You **are** a student. We **are** students. They **are** students.
Junko **is** a student. She **is** a student. My sister **is** a student.
Amir **is** a boxer. Sultan **is** a farmer. My grandfather **is** a doctor.
London **is** a big city. It **is** a big farm. His name **is** Tom.
Angela and Ottavio **are** Italian. They **are** Italian.

1 Read the texts (A and B) and write *am, is* or *are* in the gaps.

A

My name (1)_____ Hamdan. I (2)_____
from Al Ain. I (3)_____ 19. Al Ain (4)_____
in the United Arab Emirates. My brother's
name (5)_____ Faisal. He (6)_____
older. He (7)_____ 26. My father's name
(8)_____ Ali.

B I (1)_____ Min Lee. I (2)_____ from Busan.
Busan (3)_____ in South Korea. I live with
my mother, my father and my sister. My mother
and father (4)_____ from Seoul. My sister
(5)_____ Hani. She (6)_____ 17. She
(7)_____ a student. Her hobbies (8)_____
swimming and watching TV.

Personal pronouns

We use *personal pronouns* before a verb. Personal pronouns are *I, you, he, she, it, we* and *they*. The pronouns *he, she, it,* and *they* can also replace nouns.

I am Min Lee.
Faisal is 26. **He** is 26. [*He* = Faisal]
Hani is a student. **She** is a student. [*She* = Hani]
Busan is a city in South Korea. **It** is a city in South Korea.
[*It* = Busan]
We are from Al Ain.
Min and Hani are from Busan. **They** are from Busan.
[*They* = Min and Hani]

2 Write the words from the box in the correct places in the table below.

grandfather   mother   sons   brother   aunts
daughter   father   uncles   sisters

she	
he	
they	

3 Read the sentences (1–4) below and write the words from the box in the gaps.

He   She   It   They

1 My sister is very tall. _____ is 175 cm.
2 My family is Egyptian. _____ are from Cairo.
3 My uncle likes swimming. _____ swims every day.
4 Paris is in France. _____ is a big city.

Possessive determiners

Possessive determiners are *my, your, his, her, its, our* and *their*. We use possessive determiners before a noun.

My family is from London.   My city is famous for its university.
Your school is in Alexandria.   Our uncle is in Dubai.
His family is from Pakistan.   Their sister is a teacher.
Her father is from Rome.

4 Read the sentences (1–5) below and write the words from the box in the gaps.

My   Her   His   Our   Their

1 I have two sisters. _____ names are Frances and Celia.
2 Jenny Fielding is from London. _____ father's name is David.
3 We go to school in Barcelona. _____ school is very big.
4 I have a brother and a sister. _____ sister's name is Aysha.
5 Amir Khan is from Bolton. _____ mother is from Pakistan.

ACADEMIC WRITING SKILLS

Punctuation

The first word in a sentence begins with a *capital letter (A, B, C)*. A sentence ends with a *full stop (.)*.

Teachers work in schools.

For some words, the first letter is always a capital letter.

names of people: My brother's name is Orhan.
names of places: Istanbul is a big city in Turkey.
the pronoun *I*: I have two sisters.

1 Put the words in order to make sentences.

1 Zhong Shan / My grandfather / is / .

_____

2 is / He / 59 / . _____

3 a doctor / He / is / . _____

4 is from / He / Hong Kong / .

_____

5 two daughters / He / has / .

_____

6 my mother and father / lives with / He / .

_____

2 Correct the punctuation in the sentences (1–10) below. Add capital letters and full stops.

1 my name is mohammed _____

2 i am from kuwait _____

3 i am 19 _____

4 my father's name is asif _____

5 he is a teacher _____

6 he has two sons _____

7 my brother's name is faran

_____

8 faran is a doctor

_____

9 he lives in canada

_____

10 faran's hobbies are swimming and watching TV

_____

WRITING TASK

Write about somebody in your family.

UNLOCK ONLINE

1 Look at the family tree you drew in the Critical Thinking section. Choose somebody from your family tree to write about.

PLAN

2 Write a profile for the person.

1 First name	
2 Last name	
3 Date of birth	
4 City	
5 Country	
6 Languages	
7 Job	
8 Family	

3 Write sentences about the person. Use the words in the table below to help you.

A	B	C
My brother's name My uncle's name My aunt's name His family Her family My family She He They We	is are	Ahmad. Tomoko. a doctor. a student. from Cairo. from Bangkok. 22. 35. 49.
	lives with	my uncle. my mother and father.
	speaks	Turkish. English. Arabic and English.

4 Use the task checklist to review your sentences.

TASK CHECKLIST	✔
Does the first word in your sentences begin with a capital letter?	
Do your sentences have full stops?	
Do people's name and places have capital letters?	
Are the personal pronouns *he* and *she* before the verb *is*?	
Are the personal pronouns *we* and *they* before the verb *are*?	
Are the possessive determiners (*my, his, her*) before a noun (*brother, sister, uncle*)?	

5 Make any necessary changes to your sentences.

OBJECTIVES REVIEW

6 Check your objectives.

I can ...

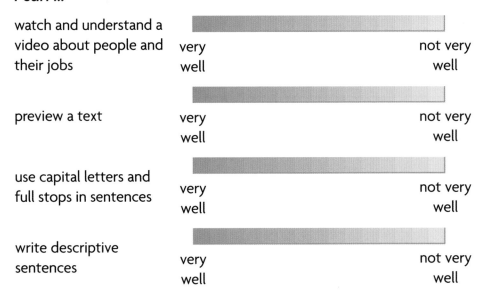

| watch and understand a video about people and their jobs | very well | not very well |

| preview a text | very well | not very well |

| use capital letters and full stops in sentences | very well | not very well |

| write descriptive sentences | very well | not very well |

WORDLIST

UNIT VOCABULARY		
aunt (n)	farmer (n)	son (n)
beautiful (adj)	grandfather (n)	tall (adj)
brother (n)	grandmother (n)	teacher (n)
clothes (n)	height (n)	uncle (n)
daughter (n)	interesting (adj)	work (v)
different (adj)	live (v)	young (adj)
famous (adj)	shoe (n)	

LEARNING OBJECTIVES

Watch and listen	Watch and understand a video about a blizzard
Reading skills	Scan a text to find information
Academic writing skills	Use capital letters in words and sentences
Writing task	Write facts

SEASONS UNIT 2

UNLOCK YOUR KNOWLEDGE

Work with a partner. Look at the words for seasons in the box and answer the questions below.

spring   summer   autumn   winter
the dry season   the monsoon season

1 Which seasons do you have in your country?
2 Which is your favourite season? Why?

WATCH AND LISTEN

PREPARING TO WATCH

UNDERSTANDING
KEY VOCABULARY

1 You are going to watch a video about weather. Before you watch, match the words in the box to the correct photographs (1–3).

> a snowstorm   snow   a snowflake

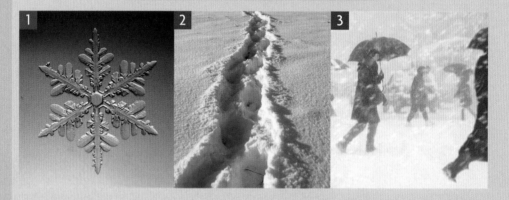

WHILE WATCHING

USING VISUALS TO
PREDICT CONTENT

2 ▶ Watch the first part of a video about weather and circle the correct option (a–c).

A blizzard is a kind of
a forest
b storm
c mountain

3 Write the words from the box in the gaps.

> close   winds   see   tall   dangerous   snow   cold   forests

1 The air is _____ .
2 There are _____ mountains and thick _____ .
3 There is a lot of _____ – 15 metres!
4 A blizzard is a snowstorm with strong _____ .
5 A blizzard is _____ .
6 Many roads _____ .
7 Drivers can't _____ .

4 ⏵ Watch the first part of the video again and check your answers.

5 ⏵ Watch the next part of the video and write true (T) or false (F) next to the statements (1–6) below.

1 The big white cloud is a blizzard. _____
2 There is a lot of snow in the mountains and forests. _____
3 The man's car is not very good. _____
4 The car stops near a city. _____
5 The man eats apples in the car. _____
6 A policeman finds the man. _____

DISCUSSION

6 Work with a partner. Use the information in Exercise 5 to answer the questions.

questions	student A	student B
Can you describe the weather in the northwest United States?	Ask	Answer
What's a blizzard? Is it dangerous?	Answer	Ask

READING 1

PREPARING TO READ

UNDERSTANDING
KEY VOCABULARY

1 Look at the words in bold and match sentences (1–4) to sentences (a–d). Use the glossary on page 194 to help you.

1	Two **plus** two is four.	**a**	It is not **difficult**.
2	Sara is **happy**.	**b**	It is **warm** in summer.
3	'2 + 2 = 4' is **easy**.	**c**	She is not **sad**.
4	Canada is **cold** in winter.	**d**	Two **minus** two is zero.

2 Match the words (1–7) to the correct numbers (a–g).

1	twenty-one	**a**	55
2	eleven	**b**	18
3	eighteen	**c**	2012
4	fifty-five	**d**	42
5	forty-two	**e**	21
6	two thousand and twelve	**f**	11
7	fifty	**g**	50

PREVIEWING

3 Look at the graph, photographs and headings in the text on the opposite page and write true (T) or false (F) next to the statements (1–4) below.

1 Yakutsk is a city.   ____
2 Winter is very cold in Yakutsk.   ____
3 Summer is very cold in Yakutsk.   ____
4 Svetlana has a café in Moscow.   ____

4 Look at the graph. Translate *Average temperatures in Yakutsk* into your language.
Translation: _____

5 Use the glossary on page 194 to check your translation.

WHILE READING

6 Match the facts (1–6) to the correct numbers (a–f).

SCANNING TO
FIND INFORMATION

UNLOCK
ONLINE

1	the average temperature in summer	**a**	–42 °C
2	the writer went to Yakutsk	**b**	2012
3	the average temperature in winter	**c**	5
4	Daria's age	**d**	–55 °C
5	the temperature when kindergartens and schools are closed	**e**	+20 °C
6	the average temperature in spring and autumn	**f**	–21 °C

Scanning to find information

Scanning means looking for information. When we scan, we do not read every word in a text. We can scan for:

- numbers
- names of people
- names of places.

Look for capital letters to find people and places.

The Coldest City in the World

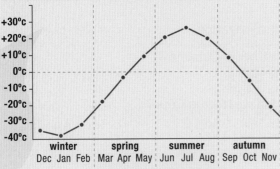

Average temperatures in Yakutsk
(December – November)

Yakutsk in winter

The temperature in your freezer is about –18 °C. Yakutsk in Russia is colder than your freezer. In winter, the average temperature is –42 °C!

In 2012, I visited Yakutsk. Why? Because I wanted to see the coldest city in the world. I wanted to meet the people of Yakutsk.

'Life is difficult in winter,' says Svetlana, 'but we're not sad.' Svetlana is the manager of a café in Yakutsk. She has two children. Her son Pavel is 11. Her daughter Daria is 5.

'The average temperature in winter is –42 °C. Some winters are colder. At –50 °C, the kindergarten is closed. Daria is happy. At –55 °C, the kindergarten and the school are closed. Daria and Pavel are happy,' Svetlana says.

People in Yakutsk like sport. In spring and autumn, the average temperature is –21 °C. They go skiing and ice-skating. In summer, it is warm. The average temperature is +20 °C. They have picnics in the forests.

Svetlana has a warm café in a cold city.

DISCUSSION

7 Work with a partner. Ask and answer the questions (1–4) below.

1 Is life easy in Yakutsk?
2 Is winter cold in your country?
3 How hot is the summer in your country?
4 Do you like hot summers or cold winters? Why?

READING 2

PREPARING TO READ

PREVIEWING

1 Look at the texts. Circle the correct answers (a–c) to the questions (1–3).

1 Where are the texts from?
   a a book   **b** a magazine   **c** a web page

2 Which text is about the weather in Cuba now?
   a Text A   **b** Text B   **c** Text C

3 Which texts are about typical weather in Cuba?
   a Texts A and B   **b** Texts B and C   **c** Texts A and C

UNDERSTANDING
KEY VOCABULARY

2 Read the sentences (1–4) below and write the words from the box in the gaps.

> wind speed   rainfall   climate   temperature

1 Use degrees centigrade (°C) to talk about _____ .
2 Use kilometres per hour (kph) to talk about _____ .
3 Use millimetres (mm) to talk about _____ .
4 Use seasons to talk about _____ .

3 Write the words from the box in the gaps in Text B opposite. Use the wordlist on page 194 to help you.

> windy   sunny   rainy   cloudy

A

CUBA WEATHER   HOME | WEATHER | CUBAN CLIMATE | WEATHER AVERAGES

Cuba is in the Caribbean. The climate in Cuba is good. It has two seasons: the dry season and the rainy season. The dry season and the rainy season last for six months.

The dry season is from November to April. The average temperatures are between 22 °C and 25 °C in the dry season. The average rainfall is 62 mm in the dry season. It is windy in the dry season.

The rainy season is from May to October. In the rainy season, the average temperatures are between 26 °C and 28 °C. The average rainfall in the rainy season is 146 mm.

The best time to visit Cuba is April or May.

B

CUBA WEATHER   HOME | WEATHER | CUBAN CLIMATE | WEATHER AVERAGES

TODAY | TOMORROW | 5 DAY | MONTHLY

TODAY	MONDAY	TUESDAY	WEDNESDAY	THURSDAY
(1) _____	cloudy and (2) _____	(3) _____ and cloudy	sunny and (4) _____	sunny
29 °C	28 °C	26 °C	29 °C	31 °C

C

CUBA WEATHER   HOME | WEATHER | CUBAN CLIMATE | WEATHER AVERAGES

SEASON (MONTHS)	AVERAGE TEMPERATURE °C	AVERAGE RAINFALL (MM)	AVERAGE WIND SPEED (KPH)
Dry (Nov–Apr)	23 °C	62 mm	8 kph
Rainy (May–Oct)	27 °C	146 mm	15 kph

WHILE READING

SCANNING TO
FIND INFORMATION

4 Match the facts (1–8) to the correct words and numbers (a–h).

1	average temperatures (°C) in the dry season	**a**	15
2	months in the rainy season	**b**	31
3	average rainfall (mm) in the dry season	**c**	22–25
4	temperature (°C) on Thursday	**d**	146
5	months in the dry season	**e**	November to April
6	average wind speed (kph) in the rainy season	**f**	62
7	average rainfall (mm) in the rainy season	**g**	26–28
8	average temperatures (°C) in the rainy season	**h**	May to October

DISCUSSION

5 Work with a partner. Ask and answer the questions below.

1 Is the climate in Cuba good?
2 What are the seasons in Cuba?
3 Is the climate in your country good?
4 What are the seasons in your country?
5 Where can you find facts about climate in your country?

⊙ LANGUAGE DEVELOPMENT

EXPLANATION

Adjectives and nouns

Words for people, places or things are *nouns*. Words that describe people, places and things are *adjectives*. Adjectives can describe states (e.g. the weather).

The man is tall. The room is cold. The climate is good.
It is hot. It is cloudy. It is sunny.

1 Circle the adjectives and underline the nouns in the sentences (1–5) below.

1 The café is warm.
2 Life is difficult.
3 The climate is good.
4 Summers are hot.
5 Winters are cold.

2 Read the sentences (1–5) below and write the words from the box in the gaps.

weather   is   brother   are   sunny

1 The school _____ closed.
2 The children _____ happy.
3 It is warm and _____ today.
4 The _____ is cold in Yakutsk.
5 My _____ is young.

EXPLANATION

Noun phrases

One type of *noun phrase* is an adjective + a noun.

noun phrases: He *is a* **tall man**. This is a **cold room**. Spain has a **good climate**. Egypt has **dry weather**. The **average rainfall** is 62 mm.

3 Make a noun phrase from the bold words in each sentence (1–4) and write it in the gaps to make a new sentence.

1 Svetlana's **café** is **warm**.
   Svetlana has a _____ _____ .
2 **Life** is **difficult** in winter.
   People have a _____ _____ in winter.
3 In Cuba, the **climate** is **good**.
   Cuba has a _____ _____ .
4 **Summers** are **warm** in Mongolia.
   Mongolia has _____ _____ .

4 Work with a partner. Correct the mistakes in the sentences (1–5) below.

1 Cuba has a climate good.

   _____

2 I have a family happy.

   _____

3 In summer, we have weather good.

   _____

4 The season is dry is from June to November.

   _____

5 The rainfall is average is 78 mm in spring.

   _____

CRITICAL THINKING

At the end of this unit, you will write facts. Look at this unit's writing task in the box below.

> Write facts about the weather in your city.

Understand a table

A *table* shows facts and numbers. It is easy to see facts and numbers in a table.

Decimal numbers have a full stop in them – for example, 1.1, 1.7, 2.7. When we say decimal numbers, we use the word *point*.

1.1 one **point** one   1.7 one **point** seven   2.7 two **point** seven

Average temperatures and rainfall in Ulaanbaatar, Mongolia

month	average temperatures (°C)	average rainfall (mm)
January	−22	1.1
February	−16	1.7
March	−7	2.7
April	+2	8.3
May	+10	13
June	+15	42
July	+19	58
August	+18	52
September	+8	26
October	0	6.4
November	−11	3.2
December	−19	2.5

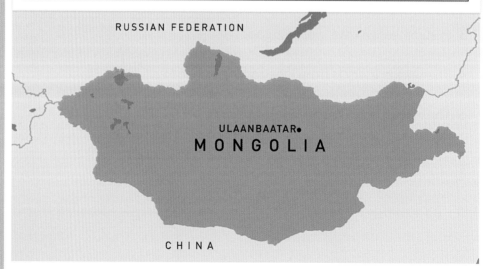

RUSSIAN FEDERATION

ULAANBAATAR•

MONGOLIA

CHINA

1 Work with a partner. Look at the table. Ask and answer the questions (1–5) below.

1 Is it rainy in February?
2 Is it dry in August?
3 Is it cold in April?
4 Is it cold in October?
5 Is summer rainy or dry?

2 Read the text below and write information from the table in the gaps.

APPLY

The weather in Ulaanbaatar

Ulaanbaatar is in (1)_____ . Ulaanbaatar has four seasons. The seasons are winter, spring, summer and autumn.

Winter is from December to February. Winters are cold in Ulaanbaatar. The average temperatures are from (2)_____ °C to −22 °C. In winter, the average (3)_____ is from (4)_____ mm to 2.5 mm.

Summer is from June to August. Summers are warm in Ulaanbaatar. In summer, the average (5)_____ are from +15 °C to (6)_____ °C. It is very rainy in summer. The (7)_____ rainfall is from (8)_____ mm to 58 mm.

WRITING

GRAMMAR FOR WRITING

Subject and verb

A sentence is about a *subject*. The subject is a *pronoun*, a *noun* or a *noun phrase*.

pronoun: I am from Beijing. She is a student. It is sunny.
noun: My father is old. Yakutsk is in Russia. The weather is cold.
noun phrase: The average rainfall is 21 mm. Typical teenagers are students.

The *verb* is after the subject in a sentence.

I am from Beijing. She is a student. It is sunny.
My father is old. Yakutsk is in Russia. The weather is cold.
The average rainfall is 21 mm. Typical teenagers are students.

UNLOCK
ONLINE

1 Match the sentence halves.

1	Svetlana	a	**is** 15 kph.
2	Jakarta	b	**are** from Cuba.
3	The average wind speed	c	**are** closed.
4	The schools	d	**is** a manager.
5	Alberto and Ana-Maria	e	**is** a big city.

Prepositions

The words *at, in, from* and *to* are examples of *prepositions*.

2 Read the sentences (1–5) below and write the prepositions from the box in the gaps.

to (x2)   from (x2)   in (x4)

1 Ulaanbaatar is _____ Mongolia.
2 Winters are cold _____ Ulaanbaatar.
3 The average temperatures are _____ –16 °C _____ –22 °C.
4 _____ summer, the average temperatures are _____ +15 °C _____ +19 °C.
5 It is very rainy _____ summer.

EXPLANATION

Prepositional phrases

A *prepositional phrase* is a preposition + a noun.

One type of prepositional phrase is a preposition + a noun for a place.

where: My brother lives in Abu Dhabi. My sister is a student in Tai Pei. I am from Ankara.

Another type of prepositional phrase is a preposition + a noun for a season or a month.

when: It is warm in summer. It is cold in January.

3 Circle the *when* prepositional phrase in the sentences (1–2) below.

  1 In the dry season, the average temperatures are between 22 ˚C and 25 ˚C.

  2 The average temperatures are between 22 ˚C and 25 ˚C in the dry season.

4 Look at the sentences in Exercise 3. Which sentence has a comma (,) after the prepositional phrase?

5 Write the prepositional phrases from the box in the gaps. Add commas and capital letters if necessary.

in July   in winter   in the monsoon season

  1 It is cold in New York _____ .

  2 _____ the average rainfall is 6 mm.

  3 The average rainfall is 360 mm _____ .

6 Put the words in order to make sentences.

  1 windy / October / , / is / it / In / .

  _____

  2 weather / good / summer / is / The / in / .

  _____

  3 Cuba / climate / good / the / is / In / , / .

  _____

  4 average / the / 34 mm / In / , / autumn / rainfall / is / .

  _____

  5 Yakutsk / The / are / cold / winters / in / .

  _____

  6 monsoon / in / season / the / is / The / temperature / average / 27 ˚C / .

  _____

  7 dry / the / season / 7 mm / In / rainfall / , / is / average / the / .

  _____

ACADEMIC WRITING SKILLS

EXPLANATION

Punctuation

Capital letters

For the following types of words, the first letter is always a *capital letter*.

names of months: April, May, June
names of days: Monday, Tuesday, Wednesday
nationalities: British, Egyptian, Korean
names of people: Ahmad, Orhan, Ryoko
names of places: Turkey, Cairo, London

1 Write the correct letters in the gaps to complete the months.

J a n __ __ r __	J u __ __
F __ b __ __ a __ y	A __ g __ s __
M a __ __ __	S e __ t e __ __ e __
A p __ __ l	O __ t __ b e r
M __ __	N o __ e __ __ e r
J __ n __	D e __ e __ __ e r

2 Correct the punctuation in the sentences below. Add capital letters, commas and full stops.

1 in january the weather is cold in russia
2 the average temperature is 21 °C in july
3 in the monsoon season the average rainfall is 315 mm in bangalore in india
4 the weather is sunny on tuesday
5 sultan lives in sharjah in the united arab emirates

WRITING TASK

Write facts about the weather in your city.

PLAN

1 Circle the correct seasons for your city.

a the dry season and the rainy season
b the dry season and the monsoon season
c spring, summer, autumn and winter

2 Write the name of one season in two or more rows in Column A.

A	B	C	D
seasons	months	average temperatures (°C)	average rainfall (mm)

3 Write the names of the months for each season in column B.

4 Write the average temperatures for each season in column C. Use the internet to help you find information.

5 Write the average rainfall for each season in column D. Use the internet to help you find information.

6 Look at the Critical Thinking section and read the text about Ulaanbaatar again.

WRITE A FIRST DRAFT

7 Write information about your city in the gaps below.

_____ (*your city*) is in _____
(*your country*). _____ (*your city*) has
_____ (*number*) seasons. The seasons are
_____ and _____ .

8 Write sentences about your city.

1 Write a sentence about the weather in one season (e.g. *It is windy/ cold/rainy*) and say which months the season is in (e.g *April, May*).
2 Write a sentence about the average temperatures in this season.
3 Write a sentence about the average rainfall in this season.
4 Write a sentence about the weather in another season (e.g. *It is windy/ cold/rainy*).
5 Write a sentence about the average temperatures in this season.
6 Write a sentence about the average rainfall in this season.

9 Use the task checklist to review your sentences.

TASK CHECKLIST	✔
Do your sentences describe two seasons?	
Do your sentences show the average temperature and rainfall?	
Do the names for your city, country and months have capital letters?	
Does the first word in your sentences begins with a capital letter?	
Do your sentences have full stops?	

10 Make any necessary changes to your sentences.

OBJECTIVES REVIEW

11 Check your objectives.

I can ...

watch and understand a video about a blizzard

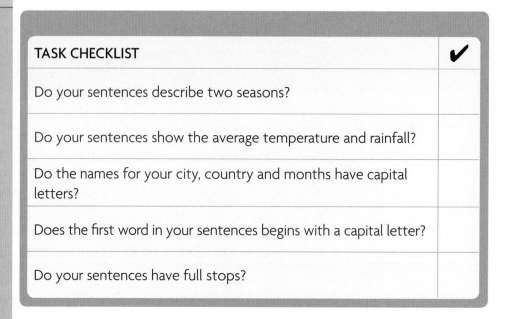

very well   not very well

scan a text to find information

very well   not very well

use capital letters in words and sentences

very well   not very well

write facts

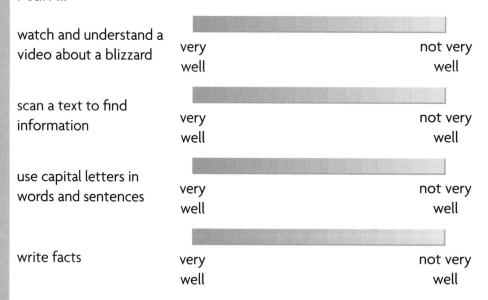

very well   not very well

WORDLIST

UNIT VOCABULARY		
autumn (n)	easy (adj)	summer (n)
cloudy (adj)	happy (adj)	sunny (adj)
cold (adj)	rainy (adj)	temperature (n)
dangerous (adj)	sad (adj)	warm (adj)
difficult (adj)	safe (adj)	windy (adj)
dry (adj)	spring (n)	winter (n)

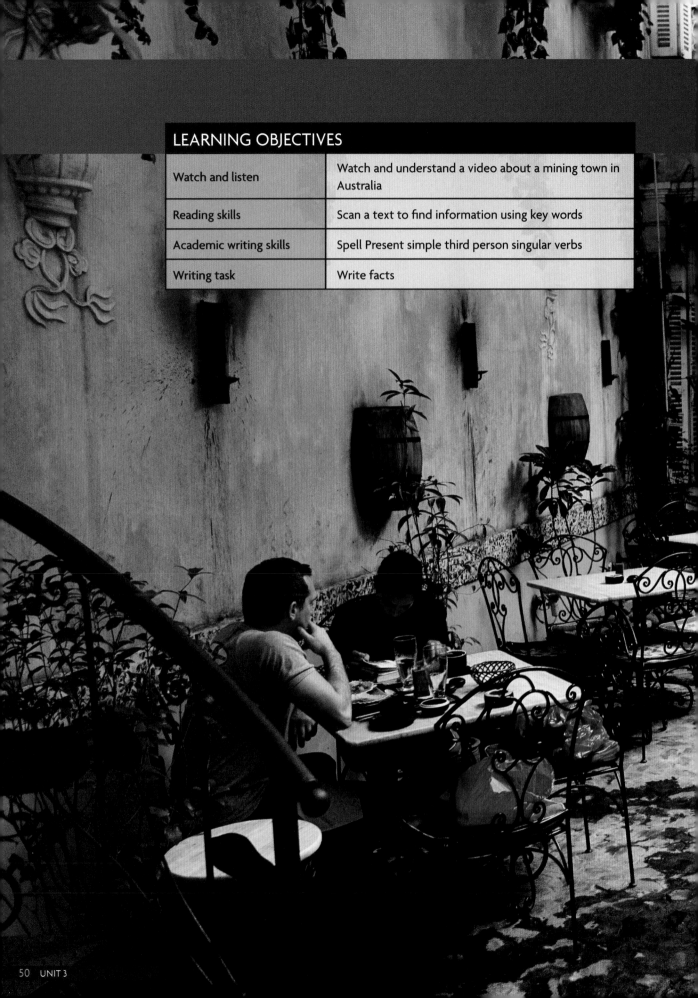

LEARNING OBJECTIVES

Watch and listen	Watch and understand a video about a mining town in Australia
Reading skills	Scan a text to find information using key words
Academic writing skills	Spell Present simple third person singular verbs
Writing task	Write facts

UNL⌀CK YOUR KNOWLEDGE

1 Write the words in the box next to the correct prepositional
phrases (1–4).

> work (x2)   study   relax with friends

1 _____ in a café
2 _____ in your room
3 _____ in a shop
4 _____ in an office

2 Work with a partner. Ask and answer the questions below.

1 Where do you study?
2 Where do you relax with friends?

PREPARING TO WATCH

UNDERSTANDING
KEY VOCABULARY

1 Check the meanings of the words in the picture. Use a dictionary to help you.

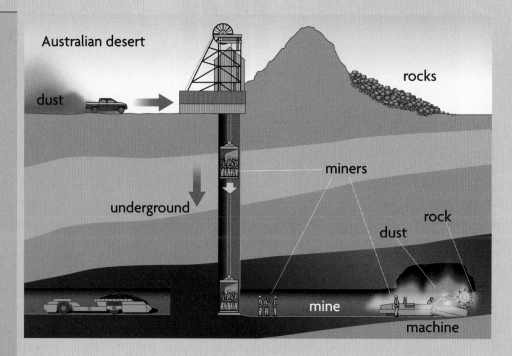

2 Read the sentences (1–6) below and write the words from the box in the gaps.

> mine   dust   rock   desert   underground   comfortable

1 There are many mines in the Australian _____ .
2 There is a lot of _____ and rock in the desert.
3 Every day, miners go to work _____ .
4 The miners cut the _____ with machines.
5 There is also a lot of dust in the _____ .
6 The mine is not a _____ place to work.

WHILE WATCHING

3 You are going to watch a video about life in a town in the Australian desert. Before you watch, read the statements (1–6) below and write true (T) or false (F) in column A.

statement	A before watching	B after watching
1 The Australian desert is very hot.		
2 The people live in tall houses.		
3 The people are on holiday.		
4 There are mines in the town.		
5 An opal is an expensive stone.		
6 People play golf at night.		

4 ⏵ Watch the video. Write true (T) or false (F) in column B.

5 ⏵ Watch again. Write the numbers from the box next to the correct facts. There are three extra numbers which you do not need.

42   55   95   3,000   5,000   50,000

1 the number of people in the town: _____
2 the price of a good opal: $ _____
3 temperatures in the desert: _____ °C

DISCUSSION

6 Work with a partner. Ask and answer the questions below.

1 Would you like to live in Coober Pedy?
2 Do you like the underground houses?
3 Is life in Coober Pedy different from life in your town or city?

READING 1

PREPARING TO READ

1 Which things in the box can you see in the text and the photographs? Circle the words. Use a dictionary to help you.

> a writer   a hunter   a jungle   a car   a tree house
> a TV   a website   a price   a book cover
> the name of a newspaper   a watch   a village

2 Read sentences (1–8) below and write the words from the box in the gaps.

> different   traditional   imagine   hunt
> amazing   lifestyle   jungle   cook

1 I like reading books, not watching movies. I like to _____ how the people look in the story.
2 I want to _____ rice for lunch.
3 Pizza is a _____ meal in Italy.
4 My _____ is not very healthy. I eat too much chocolate.
5 His daughters are very _____ . Hande is tall but Adile is small.
6 They have guns. In autumn, they _____ animals in the forest.
7 The Amazon is a big _____ in South America.
8 I love this book! The story is _____!

'This book shows you a different lifestyle.' *Daily Press*

Can you imagine your life with no mobile phones or TV? With no cars or supermarkets? Can you imagine life in a tree house?

Rebecca Moore

In her book, *A Life in the Trees*, journalist Rebecca Moore travels 15,000 km from London to Papua New Guinea. In Papua New Guinea, Rebecca meets the Kombai people. She tells the story of their traditional lifestyle.

Moore lived with the Kombai women and children for three months. Kombai life is very different. They have no watches and no cars. The Kombai get up every morning at sunrise.

Kombai men hunt in the jungle. They can hunt in the jungle for 12 hours. They bring meat to the village. The Kombai also eat cucumbers, mushrooms and green bananas. The women cook. There is no school for the children. Parents teach their children the traditional lifestyle of their people.

The most important part of Kombai life is building their amazing tree houses. The men, women and children all help to build a tree house. Each house is 20 m high. The stories of the Kombai people are amazing.

'Buy this book!'
Jeffrey Rost,
Lifestyle

'It has amazing photographs on every page.'
Simon Higgins,
New Look

Kombai tree house

Kombai hunter

Price   UK £10.99

WHILE READING

3 Read the text again and put a tick in the correct boxes. The first one has been done for you as an example.

	Rebecca Moore	Kombai men	Kombai women	Kombai children
1 hunt animals in the jungle		✓		
2 travels 15,000 km				
3 cook				
4 eat green bananas				
5 have no cars				
6 teach children the traditional lifestyle				
7 build tree houses				
8 tells the story of the traditional Kombai lifestyle				

EXPLANATION

Pronouns and possessive determiners

I, you, he, she, it, we and *they* are personal pronouns. *My, your, his, her, its* and *their* are possessive determiners. We use *possessive determiners* before a noun. We can use some *personal pronouns* (*he, she, it,* and *they*) to replace nouns.

You can match personal pronouns and possessive determiners to nouns to help you understand a text.

Faisal has a new mobile phone. It [*It* = new mobile phone] is amazing.
He [*He* = Faisal] uses it [*it* = new mobile phone] every day.
Kamile has a new car. Her car [*Her car* = Kamile's car] is amazing.
Her sister [*Her sister* = Kamile's sister] has a bicycle.

4 Match sentences (1–4) to sentences (a–d). Look at the pronouns to help you.

1 In Papua New Guinea, Rebecca meets the Kombai people.
2 The men can hunt in the jungle for 12 hours.
3 Kombai people have a very different lifestyle.
4 The book is called *A Life in the Trees*.

a They bring meat to the village.
b She tells the story of their traditional lifestyle.
c 'It has amazing photographs on every page.' Simon Higgins, *New Look*
d They have no watches and no cars.

5 Read the text again to check your answers.

READING 2

PREPARING TO READ

1 Write the words from the box in the correct places in the table below. Use the glossary on page 195 to help you.

UNDERSTANDING KEY VOCABULARY

> evening   Maths   get up   busy   Tuesday   quiet
> Engineering   Friday   take   Monday   study   late
> Wednesday   early   morning   relax   afternoon   Physics

verb	adjective	name of a subject	part of the day	day of the week

2 Look at the timetable and the text on the next page. Write true (T) or false (F) next to the statements (1–3).

PREVIEWING

1 The timetable is for an Engineering student.   ____
2 The timetable and the text are from a website.   ____
3 The text and the timetable are about Abdullah Taha.   ____

WHILE READING

**SCANNING TO
FIND INFORMATION**

3 Read the timetable and the text again. Circle the correct key words to
make true sentences about Abdullah.

Abdullah ...

1 <u>relaxes</u> with friends every *evening* / *Thursday evening*.
2 is a <u>student</u> in *Cairo* / *Riyadh*.
3 says that his <u>life</u> is *busy* / *quiet*.
4 has *three* / *five* classes <u>every morning</u>.
5 goes to the *Camera Club* / *gym* on <u>Wednesday evening</u>.
6 studies <u>Maths</u> every *morning* / *afternoon*.
7 <u>gets up</u> *late* / *early*.
8 <u>takes</u> *three* / *five* courses at the university.
9 has <u>Arabic History</u> class on *Tuesday* / *Thursday*.
10 <u>studies</u> in the <u>Faculty</u> of *Engineering* / *English*.

Name of student: *Abdullah Taha*   **Department:** *Faculty of Engineering*

morning						Fri	Sat
	Sun	**Mon**	**Tue**	**Wed**	**Thur**		
8–9 am	*Physics 101 lecture*	*Physics seminar*	*Physics 101 lecture*	*Physics 101*	*Physics 101 lecture*		
9.15–10.15 am	*Maths 121*	*Maths 121 lecture*	*Maths 121*	*Maths 121 lecture*	*Maths 121 seminar*		
10.30–11.30 am	*Engineering 122 lecture*	*Engineering 122 seminar*	*Engineering 122 lecture*	*Engineering 122*	*Engineering 122 lecture*		

afternoon						Fri	Sat
	Sun	**Mon**	**Tue**	**Wed**	**Thur**		
12.30–1.30 pm	*Study group*						
2–3 pm		*English 101*	*Library*	*English 101*	*Arabic History 123 lecture*		

evening						Fri	Sat
	Sun	**Mon**	**Tue**	**Wed**	**Thur**		
5–7 pm	*Library*	*Library*	*Library*	*Library*	*Relax with friends*		
7–10 pm	*Library*	*Library*	*Camera Club*	*Go to the gym*	*Relax with friends*		

Abdullah Taha

Abdullah Taha is a student in my class. This is his timetable. Abdullah studies Engineering at Cairo University. Abdullah takes five courses. They are Physics, Maths, English, Engineering and Arabic History. His favourite subjects are Physics and Maths.

Abdullah is a serious student. He gets up at 6 am every day. He studies every evening. He has many classes, seminars and lectures every week.

Abdullah has three classes every morning. He has Physics from 8 am to 9 am, Maths from 9.15 am to 10.15 am, and Engineering from 10.30 am to 11.30 am.

On Sunday, he meets his study group. His study group is from 12.30 pm to 1.30 pm. On Monday and Wednesday, he has English. His English class is from 2 pm to 3 pm. On Thursday afternoon, he has Arabic History from 2 pm to 3 pm.

In the evening, Abdullah studies in the library. In his free time, Abdullah relaxes with friends. Sometimes, Abdullah goes to the cinema. Abdullah likes taking photographs. He is in the University Camera Club.

Abdullah says, 'My university life is very busy. I have a lot of exams and projects, but I always have time to relax with friends and family.'

DISCUSSION

4 Work with a partner. Ask and answer the questions below.

1 Do you go to university?
2 Do you get up late or early?
3 Is your lifestyle the same as or different from Abdullah's?
4 Do you relax with friends or family in the evening?
5 Are you in a club?

⦿ LANGUAGE DEVELOPMENT

EXPLANATION

Collocations

A pair or small group of words which are often used together is a *collocation*. One type of collocation is a verb + a noun or a verb + a noun phrase.

I **have breakfast** [have + breakfast]. Dae-Jung and Chung-Hee **play video games** [play + video games]. Abdullah **studies Maths** [study + Maths].

Another type of collocation is a verb + a prepositional phrase.

Abdullah **goes to the cinema** [goes + to the cinema]. Abdullah **studies in the library** [studies + in the library]. Abdullah **relaxes with friends** [relaxes + with friends].

1 Match the sentence halves.

1 Eun Jung **studies**	a **coffee** for breakfast.
2 Asif **gets up**	b **Maths** at Cambridge University.
3 Melody and Ginger **take**	c **early**.
4 In the morning, **I have**	d **to the cinema** every Saturday.
5 My friends **go**	e **the bus** every morning.

2 Read the sentences (1–10) below and write the verbs from the box in the gaps.

> do   have   live   relax   go (x2)   reads   has   eats   cooks

1 I _____ with my parents.
2 Sultan _____ a **shower** at 7 am every morning.
3 You _____ **to the gym** every day.
4 My grandfather _____ a **newspaper** every morning.
5 Melody and Ginger _____ **breakfast** on the bus!
6 Li Mei _____ **her lunch** in the café.
7 Viraj and Dhirendra _____ **with friends** in the evenings.
8 You _____ **your homework** in the evening.
9 My sister _____ **dinner** for my family.
10 I _____ **to bed** at 11 pm.

VOCABULARY FOR STUDY

3 Read the names of the subjects. Put a tick in the correct box. Use the glossary on page 195 to help you.

subject	Arts and Humanities	Business	Science	Languages
Maths				
Physics				
Literature				
English				
Economics				
Biology				
History				
Management				
Arabic				
Geography				
Chemistry				
Art and Design				

CRITICAL THINKING

At the end of this unit, you will write facts. Look at this unit's writing task in the box below.

> Write facts about the lifestyle of a student in your class.

REMEMBER

1 Work with a partner. Ask and answer the questions (1–8) below.

1 What is your name and surname?
2 Where do you go to school/university?
3 What subjects do you study?
4 When do you get up?
5 When are your classes?
6 When do you have lunch?
7 When do you go to the library?
8 When do you relax with friends?

CREATE

2 Write your partner's answers in the timetable below.

Name of student: _____

School/University: _____

Subjects: _____

	Day 1:	Day 2:	Day 3:	Day 4:	Day 5:
morning					
lunch					
afternoon					
evening					

UNL⊘CK READING AND WRITING SKILLS 1

WRITING

GRAMMAR FOR WRITING

EXPLANATION

Subject – Verb – Object

A sentence is about a *subject*. The subject is a pronoun, a noun or a noun phrase. The verb is after the subject in a sentence.

subject: Li Mei has lunch. **My grandfather** reads a newspaper.
My sister cooks dinner.
verb: Li Mei **has** lunch. My grandfather **reads** a newspaper. My sister **cooks** dinner.

A sentence can have an *object*. The object is a pronoun, a noun or a noun phrase. The object is after the verb.

object: Li Mei eats **her lunch**. My grandfather reads a **newspaper**. My sister cooks **dinner**.

A prepositional phrase after a verb is <u>not</u> an object.

Abdullah studies **in the library**. He lives **in Cairo**.

A pronoun, a noun or a noun phrase after *is* or *are* is <u>not</u> an object.

Abdullah is **a student**. Melody and Ginger are **students**.

1 Read the sentences below. Put a tick (✔) if the bold word or phrase is an object.

1 Kombai life is **very different**.
2 Attila does **his homework** in the morning.
3 Every morning, I have a **shower**.
4 Somlek studies **Maths**.
5 Ayşe has **orange juice and coffee** in the morning.
6 Kombai men hunt **in the jungle**.
7 My teacher asks **questions**.
8 Milena Telak works **in Coober Pedy**.

2 Work with a partner. Correct the mistakes in the sentences (1–5) below.

1 The Kombai meat eat.
2 Kombai men animals hunt.
3 Books Rebecca Moore writes.
4 Abdullah in the library reads books.
5 Melody drinks in the morning coffee.

Present simple

We use the *Present simple* to talk about our typical lifestyle.

I have a shower every morning.

If the subject of the sentence is third person and singular (e.g. *he, she, it, Faisal, Kate, my cat*), we add -*s* to the verb.

He reads books. Kate listens to music. My cat likes milk.

If the verb is *go*, we add -*es*. If the verb is *have*, we use *has*.

~~Faisal gos to the cinema on Monday evenings~~. → Faisal goes to the cinema on Monday evenings.

~~My mother haves breakfast at 8 am~~. → My mother has breakfast at 8 am.

3 Read the text. Circle the correct forms of the verbs.

> Noreen [1] *is / are* a student in my class. This [2] *is / are* her timetable.
> She [3] *study / studies* English at university. She [4] *get up / gets up*
> at 6 am. She [5] *have / has* breakfast at 6.30 am. On Mondays and
> Wednesdays, Noreen [6] *have / has* a study group at 11 am. She
> [7] *have / has* lunch at 12.30 pm every day. She [8] *study / studies*
> in the library from 3 to 6 pm. She [9] *go / goes* to the cinema with
> friends on Sundays. Noreen [10] *is / are* a serious student.

Time expressions

Time expressions say when or how often something happens. One type of time expression is *every* + a noun for time.

I read a book every week. She has English class every Wednesday afternoon. They play football every morning.

Another type of time expression is a prepositional phrase for time. The type of phrase that follows the preposition shows which preposition to use.

- *at* + clock time: at 10 am, at 3 pm
- *in* + part of the day: in the morning, in the afternoon, in the evening
- *on* + day of the week: on Monday, on Tuesdays
- *on* + day of the week + part of the day: on Monday morning, on Tuesday afternoon, on Friday evening, on Sunday night

4 Write *at*, *in* or *on* in the gaps.

1 Simon plays tennis _____ Saturday morning _____ 8 am.
2 _____ the evening, Abdullah studies in the library.
3 _____ Monday, I have English class _____ 2 pm.
4 I talk to my family _____ the evening.
5 _____ Tuesday morning, David has Maths _____ 11 am.
6 Aftab goes to university _____ Monday and Thursday.
7 I do my homework _____ the evening.
8 My father goes to work _____ 7 am every day.

ACADEMIC WRITING SKILLS

Spelling

In the alphabet, the *vowels* are *a, e, i, o* and *u*. The other letters are *consonants*. To make the third person singular form of a verb in the Present simple, we need to follow spelling rules.

- We add -*s* if the verb ends in a consonant (e.g. rea**d** → rea**ds**) or a consonant sound (e.g. writ**e** → writ**es**).
- We replace -*y* with -*ies* if the verb ends in a consonant + -*y* (e.g. stu**dy** → stud**ies**)
- We add -*es* if the verb ends in a vowel (e.g. g**o** → go**es**)
- We add -*s* if the verb ends in a vowel + -*y* (e.g. sa**y** → say**s**)

Some verbs are irregular (e.g. ha**ve** → has, **be** → is)

1 Write the third person singular form of the Present simple verb.

infinitive	third person singular
get up	
sell	
go	
study	
pay	
have	

2 Put the letters in the correct order to make the names of subjects. Use the glossary on page 195 to help you.

1 ahtms   M_____
2 snegihl   E_____
3 siphcsy   P_____
4 regeingnine   E_____
5 ryshito   H_____
6 lobiogy   B_____
7 grgephyoa   G_____

WRITING TASK

> Write facts about the lifestyle of a student in your class.

1 Look at the timetable you made in the Critical Thinking section.

2 Look at the sentences below and write answers in the gaps that are true for your partner.

_____ (*student's name*) is a student in my class.

This is _____ (*his/her*) timetable.

3 Write sentences that are true for your partner.

1 Write a sentence about the subject(s) he/she studies.
2 Write a sentence about the time he/she gets up.
3 Write four sentences about his/her school or university timetable.
4 Write two sentences about his/her evenings and free time.

4 Use the task checklist to review your sentences.

TASK CHECKLIST	✔
Do your sentences use the Present simple to describe your partner's lifestyle?	
Did you add -*s* to the Present simple third person?	
Do your sentences say when your partner does things (e.g. *in the evening, on Monday morning,* etc.)?	
Did you use prepositional phrases at the beginning or the end of a sentence?	
Does every sentence have a subject and a verb?	
If a sentence has an object, is the object after the verb?	

5 Make any necessary changes to your sentences.

OBJECTIVES REVIEW

6 Check your objectives.

I can ...

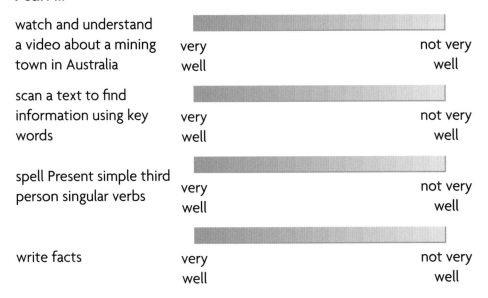

watch and understand a video about a mining town in Australia — very well / not very well

scan a text to find information using key words — very well / not very well

spell Present simple third person singular verbs — very well / not very well

write facts — very well / not very well

WORDLIST

UNIT VOCABULARY		
afternoon (n)	Engineering (n)	morning (n)
Art (n)	evening (n)	Physics (n)
Biology (n)	Friday (n)	Science (n)
Business (n)	Geography (n)	study (v)
café (n)	History (n)	Tuesday (n)
car (n)	Humanities (n)	TV (n)
Chemistry (n)	late (adj)	village (n)
cook (v)	Literature (n)	watch (n)
different (adj)	Management (n)	Wednesday (n)
early (adj)	Maths (n)	work (n and v)
Economics (n)	Monday (n)	

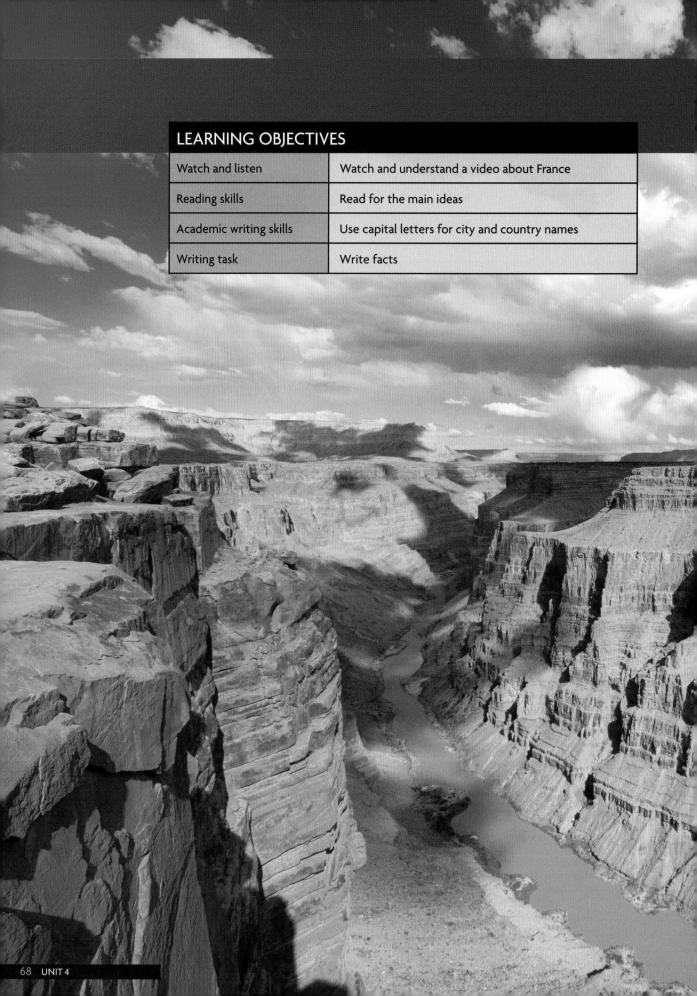

LEARNING OBJECTIVES

Watch and listen	Watch and understand a video about France
Reading skills	Read for the main ideas
Academic writing skills	Use capital letters for city and country names
Writing task	Write facts

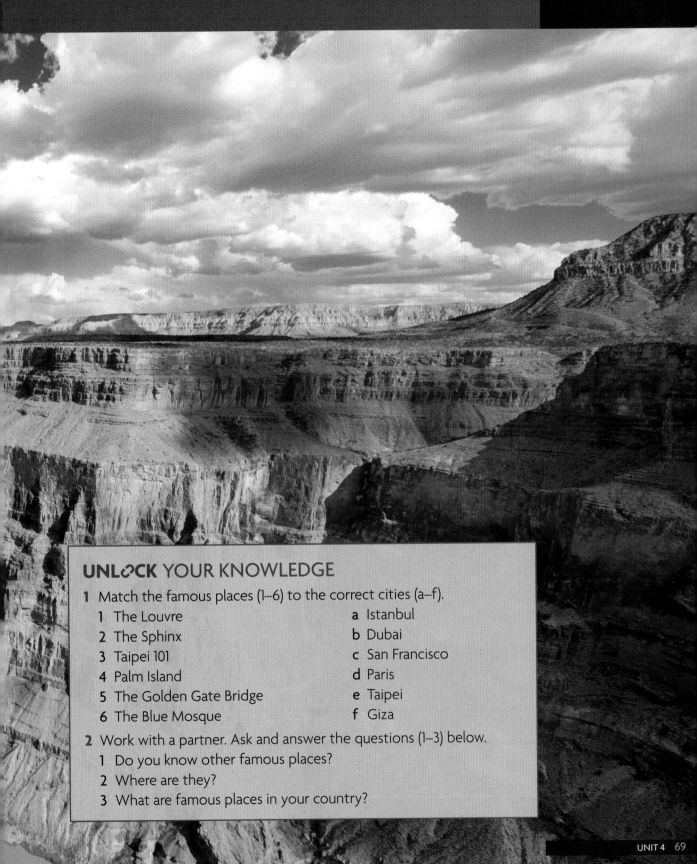

UNL⌀CK YOUR KNOWLEDGE

1 Match the famous places (1–6) to the correct cities (a–f).

1 The Louvre
2 The Sphinx
3 Taipei 101
4 Palm Island
5 The Golden Gate Bridge
6 The Blue Mosque

a Istanbul
b Dubai
c San Francisco
d Paris
e Taipei
f Giza

2 Work with a partner. Ask and answer the questions (1–3) below.

1 Do you know other famous places?
2 Where are they?
3 What are famous places in your country?

WATCH AND LISTEN

PREPARING TO WATCH

UNDERSTANDING KEY VOCABULARY

1 Write the words from the box in the gaps.

> mountains   capital city   tower   races   cheese   Tourists

1 _____ visit famous places on holiday. They take photographs.
2 Michael Phelps is a famous swimmer. He wins all his _____ .
3 My favourite lunch is bread, _____ and an apple.
4 Fuji, Jebel Hafeet, Ağrı Dağı, and Kilimanjaro are famous _____ .
5 The _____ of China is Beijing.
6 'Big Ben' is the name of a famous clock _____ in London.

USING YOUR KNOWLEDGE TO PREDICT CONTENT

2 You are going to watch a video about France. Before you watch, read the quiz questions (1–5) and circle the correct answers (a–c).

QUIZ TIME!

This week … *France*

1 Which is the French flag?

ⓐ   ⓑ   ⓒ

2 What is the capital city of France?
ⓐ Lyon
ⓑ Marseille
ⓒ Paris

3 Which of the famous places below is in Paris?
ⓐ the Galata Tower
ⓑ the Eiffel Tower
ⓒ the Sphinx

4 Which kinds of food below are famous in France?
ⓐ hamburgers and cheese
ⓑ sausages and pizza
ⓒ bread and cheese

5 Which of the mountains below are in France?
ⓐ the Alps and the Pyrenees
ⓑ the Pyrenees and the Andes
ⓒ the Andes and the Urals

WHILE WATCHING

3 ▶ Watch the video. Check your answers to the quiz in Exercise 2.

4 ▶ Watch again. Circle the numbers you hear.

> 3   20   350   450   3,000   30,000   60,000
> 6,000,000   35,000,000

5 Read the sentences (1–5) below and write the circled numbers from Exercise 4 in the gaps.

1 There are _____ colours in the French flag.
2 There are many tourists in Paris. _____ tourists visit the Eiffel Tower every year.
3 There are _____ works of art in the Louvre.
4 There are _____ different kinds of bread in France.
5 There are _____ different kinds of cheese in France.

DISCUSSION

6 Work with a partner. Ask and answer the questions (1–4) below.

1 What is the capital city of your country?
2 Are there many tourists in the capital city of your country?
3 What kinds of food are popular in your country?
4 Are there any mountains in your country?

READING 1

PREPARING TO READ

UNDERSTANDING
KEY VOCABULARY

1 Match the words (1–7) to their definitions (a–g).

1	explore	**a**	one part of the text of a book
2	table of contents	**b**	very old
3	chapter	**c**	very new
4	modern	**d**	a picture that shows countries, cities, roads,
5	discover		mountains, etc.
6	ancient	**e**	part of a book that shows the order of things
7	map	**f**	to find something
		g	to look for something

2 Read the sentences (1–6) below and write the words from the box in the gaps. Use the glossary on page 196 to help you.

> rivers   Lake   forest   Sea   Ocean   mountains

1 _____ Baikal in Russia is very big and cold.

2 There are 21 different countries on the Mediterranean

_____ .

3 The Pyrenees are _____ between France and Spain.

4 There are many trees in a _____ .

5 The Danube and the Nile are famous _____ .

6 The Pacific _____ is between America and Asia.

PREVIEWING

3 Look at the texts and the picture. Read the questions (1–3) and circle the correct answers (a–c).

1 What is the book about?
   a the history of the world
   b the history of China
   c the history of maps

2 The price of the book is:
   a $16.75
   b £16.75
   c €16.75

3 The picture shows
   a a modern map of the world
   b an ancient map of the world
   c a photograph of the world

Take a look!

Feedback | Help | Close

A World History of Maps
by J. Armour

Add to Basket

★★★★☆

Price: from £16.75

Book sections

▶ Table of contents
Introduction
Chapter 4.2

Table of contents

A World History of Maps
by J. Armour

Add to Basket

★★★★☆

Price: from £16.75

Book sections

Table of contents
Introduction
▶ Chapter 4.2

4.2

Figure 4.3: World Map by Muhammad al-Idrisi, 1154

Muhammad al-Idrisi came from Morocco. In his life, Al-Idrisi travelled to Asia, France, England and Spain.

Al-Idrisi's map of the world is called the Tabula Rogeriana in Europe. The map is in Arabic. His map helped people travel from country to country.

The map shows North Africa, Europe, and South and East Asia. There are many European countries on the map. There is Norway in the north, Spain in the west, and Italy in the south. The map also shows India and China.

There are forests, rivers, lakes, mountains, seas and oceans on the map. Al-Idrisi's map shows the Mediterranean Sea, the Indian Ocean and the river Nile.

WHILE READING

SCANNING TO
FIND INFORMATION

4 Scan the table of contents. Which chapter of the book has information about the things below?

1 maps by Pei Xiu   ____
2 maps of ancient Greece   ____
3 maps by Al-Khwarizmi   ____
4 modern maps   ____
5 maps of ancient Rome   ____

5 Scan the texts again and find the continents and countries that are mentioned. Circle them in the table below.

continents	countries
Asia	Mexico
Australia	Spain
Europe	Norway
Africa	Malaysia
America	China

READING FOR DETAIL

6 Read part of Chapter 4.2. Write true (T) or false (F) next to the statements (1–5) below.

1 Muhammad al-Idrisi was Algerian.   ____
2 *Tabula Rogeriana* is the Arabic name of Al-Idrisi's map. ____
3 America is not on the map.   ____
4 India is on the map.   ____
5 There are lakes on the map.   ____

READING 2

PREPARING TO READ

1 Circle the word in each group that is different. Use a dictionary to help you.

1 lake   river   sea   France
2 shop   road   school   factory
3 ocean   airport   harbour   train station
4 dive   drive   surf   swim

2 Match the words (1–4) to their definitions (a–d). Use a dictionary to help you.

1 currency
2 population
3 tourism
4 delicious

a very good to eat or drink
b money in a country
c the number of people in a place
d business with tourists

an international airport in the Maldives

3 Look at the headings in the text and the photographs. Circle the correct options (a–c).

1 I think this text comes from a book about
   a the history of a country.
   b the history of maps.
   c information for tourists.

2 I think a traditional kind of food in the Maldives is
   a rice.   b fish.   c beef.

3 I think a popular sport in the Maldives is
   a football.   b tennis.   c swimming.

WHILE READING

4 Read the text. Match the topics (1–8) below to the paragraphs (A–H) in the text.

1 languages   ____   5 hobbies and sports   ____
2 the population   ____   6 where the Maldives are   ____
3 a young Maldivian's home   ____   7 traditional food   ____
4 the economy   ____   8 the capital city   ____

Reading for main ideas

Many texts have *paragraphs*. A paragraph is part of a long text. Each paragraph has one topic or main idea. When we read for the main ideas in a text, we read each paragraph to find:

- the topic (e.g. family, weather, university).

- the important information about the topic (e.g. the number of brothers and sisters a person has; the average rainfall in summer; the reason a student wants to study).

Al-Idrisi's map of the world is called the *Tabula Rogeriana* in Europe. The map is in Arabic. His map helped people travel from country to country.

Al-Idrisi's map is the *topic*. The *important information about the topic* is the name of the map.

DISCUSSION

5 Work with a partner. Ask and answer the questions (1–5) below.

1 Where is your country?
2 What is the population of your country?
3 What is the capital city of your country?
4 What languages do people speak in your country?
5 What are important businesses in your country?

The Maldives
– AN OVERVIEW

A The Maldives are islands in the Indian Ocean. The islands are near Sri Lanka. The Maldives are famous for their good climate, beautiful beaches and warm seas.

B There are 360,000 people in the Maldives. Most people live on small islands.

C The capital city of the Maldives is Malé. It is a modern city with an international airport and a big harbour.

D People in Malé speak English and Dhivehi. English is useful because many tourists come here.

E Tourism and fishing are the most important businesses in the Maldives. Many people work in tourist resorts. Others work as fishermen or in fish factories. The currency is the rufiyaa.

FACT FILE

FULL NAME: Republic of Maldives

POPULATION: 360,000

CAPITAL CITY: Malé

GEOGRAPHY: 1,190 islands

CLIMATE: good, average temperature 30 °C

LANGUAGES: Dhivehi and English

RELIGION: Islam

CURRENCY: rufiyaa

INDUSTRY: tourism and fishing

ONE OF THE MALDIVES' BEAUTIFUL BEACHES

MEET THE LOCALS
Ahmed Faiz, 19

F I live on an island south of Malé. Life on my island is very simple. There are some shops and one mosque. We speak Dhivehi, but we also learn English in high school.

G The Maldives are famous for their fish. The most popular food here is *garudiya*. It's a delicious fish soup.

H People in the Maldives like to swim and dive.

AHMED FAIZ

⦿ LANGUAGE DEVELOPMENT

VOCABULARY FOR PLACES IN A CITY

1 Write the words from the box in the correct places on the picture.

> museum   train station   university   library   monument
> bridge   bank   factory   park   fountain

Noun phrases with *of*

One type of noun phrase is a noun + *of* + a noun.

Paris is the capital city of France. Paris is in the centre of the country. This book is about the history of Japan.

2 Match the sentence halves.

1 A World History   a of the United States.
2 The capital city   b of art in the Louvre.
3 The dollar is the currency   c of Belgium are Dutch and French.
4 The main languages   d of Maps.
5 There are 30,000 works   e of the Maldives is Malé.

VOCABULARY FOR PLACES IN A COUNTRY

3 Write the words from the box in the correct places on the picture.

cliff   farm   hill   desert   valley   mountains
beach   sea   field   forest

CRITICAL THINKING

At the end of this unit, you will write facts. Look at this unit's writing task in the box below.

> Write facts about your country.

Planning

Before you write, put your sentences in a *logical order*. This means putting the topics you write about in order of importance.

CREATE

1 Put the topics in the box in a logical order. Write them in column A of the table below.

> language   currency   population   religion   food
> capital city   industry   climate   full name   geography

	A the topic	B key words for the topic
1		
2		
3		
4		
5		
6		
7		
8		
9		
10		

Classifying

Classifying means putting words into groups. Each group has a topic. Classifying helps you to plan your writing.

APPLY

2 Think of key words for your country. Write the key words for each topic in column B of the table above.

WRITING

GRAMMAR FOR WRITING

EXPLANATION

there is / there are

We use *there is / there are* to say that something exists. We use *there is* before singular nouns and *there are* before plural nouns.

singular:

> There is an airport in Malé.
> There is a mosque on Ahmad Faiz's island.
> There is a famous bridge in San Francisco.

plural:

> There are 30,000 works of art in the Louvre.
> There are 350 different kinds of cheese.
> There are 360,000 people in the Maldives.

1 Put the words in order to make sentences.

1 are / in my country / different kinds / There / of business / .

   _____

2 36 / languages / in Senegal / There / are / .

   _____

3 airports / three / modern / my city / are / in / There / .

   _____

4 Seoul / There / of art / museum / in / a / is / big / .

   _____

5 palace / famous / a / There / my / in / city / is / .

   _____

2 Read the sentences (1–8) below. Put a tick if they are correct and a cross if they are wrong.

   1 There are many kinds of bread in Russia.
   2 There is a deserts in Egypt.
   3 There is many parks in London.
   4 In Thailand, there are many islands.
   5 There have many people in Jakarta.
   6 There are in Istanbul many bridges.
   7 They are many famous monuments in Rome.
   8 Is a famous museum in my city.

3 Correct the wrong sentences in Exercise 2.

Determiners: articles

We use *articles* before a noun or before an adjective + noun. There are four articles: *a, an, the* and *the zero article*.

We use *the* before the names of:

- rivers – the river Danube, the river Nile, the river Thames
- seas – the North Sea, the Mediterranean Sea, the Black Sea
- oceans – the Pacific Ocean, the Atlantic Ocean, the Indian Ocean
- many famous places – the Galata Tower, the Eiffel Tower, the Tower of London
- 'united' countries – the United Arab Emirates, the United Kingdom, the United States of America
- groups of islands – the Philippines, the Maldives, the Azores
- groups of mountains – the Andes, the Alps, the Himalayas

We use no article (*the zero article*) before the names of:

- continents – Asia, America, Europe
- countries – England, China, Turkey
- cities – Abu Dhabi, Bangkok, Shanghai

4 Read the sentences (1–6) below and write *the* or *0* (for *zero article*) in the gaps.

1 My family comes from _____ Chile.
2 _____ Chile is in _____ South America.
3 We live near _____ Pacific Ocean.
4 _____ Andes are the highest mountains in my country.
5 My sister lives in _____ United States.
6 She works in _____ Chicago.

5 Correct the mistakes in the sentences (1–7) below.

1 I come from the India.

_____

2 The Paris is popular with tourists.

_____

3 There are many tall buildings in the Abu Dhabi.

_____

4 There are 3 million people in the Nagoya in the Japan.

_____

5 United Kingdom is in the Europe.

_____

6 Many people live in the Cairo.

_____

7 Ural mountains are in Russia.

_____

ACADEMIC WRITING SKILLS

SPELLING AND PUNCTUATION

Capital letters

The first letter of the name of a city, the name of a country and the adjective for a nationality is always a *capital letter*.

1 Look at the country names and write vowels in the gaps to make the correct nationality names.

country	nationality
China	Ch__n__s__
India	__nd__ __n
Egypt	__gypt__ __n
Saudi Arabia	S__ __d__
The United Arab Emirates	__m__r__t__
Algeria	__lg__r__ __n
Japan	J__p__n__s__
Thailand	Th__ __
Turkey	T__rk__sh
France	Fr__nch
The United Kingdom	Br__t__sh
Canada	C__n__d__ __n
Chile	Ch__l__ __n

2 Correct the punctuation in the sentences (1–5) below. Add capital letters and full stops.

1 i come from abu dhabi
2 there are many beautiful fountains in rome
3 the climate is good in the maldives
4 there are four main islands in japan
5 chicken is very popular in malaysia

WRITING TASK

WRITE A FIRST DRAFT

EDIT

> Write facts about your country.

1 Read the list of topics and key words you wrote for your country in the Critical Thinking section.

2 Write two sentences for each topic. Use the key words to help you.

The capital of my country is Bangkok. There is a famous museum in Bangkok called the National Museum.
The population of Thailand is 70,000,000. There are many young people in my country.

3 Use the task checklist to review your sentences.

TASK CHECKLIST	✔
Are your sentences in a logical order?	
Did you use *the* before the names of rivers, seas, oceans, some countries and famous places?	
Did you use the no article (the zero article) before the names of continents, some countries and cities?	
Did you use *there is* … is before a singular noun?	
Did you use *there are* … is before a plural noun?	
Did you begin names for cities, countries and adjectives for nationality with a capital letter?	

4 Make any necessary changes to your sentences.

OBJECTIVES REVIEW

5 Check your objectives.

I can ...

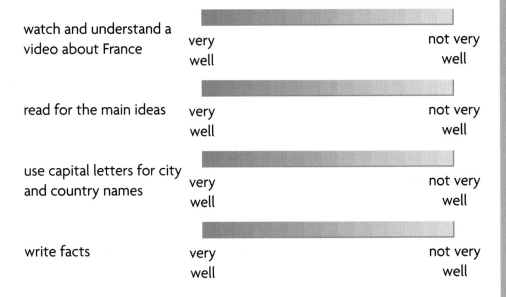

watch and understand a
video about France

very
well

not very
well

read for the main ideas

very
well

not very
well

use capital letters for city
and country names

very
well

not very
well

write facts

very
well

not very
well

WORDLIST

UNIT VOCABULARY		
bank (n)	fish (n)	river (n)
beach (n)	forest (n)	road (n)
bridge (n)	fountain (n)	school (n)
capital city (n)	hill (n)	sea (n)
cliff (n)	library (n)	shop (n)
desert (n)	monument (n)	train station (n)
factory (n)	mountain (n)	university (n)
farm (n)	museum (n)	valley (n)
field (n)	park (n)	

LEARNING OBJECTIVES

Watch and listen	Watch and understand a video about Tai-chi and Kung-fu
Reading skills	Use your knowledge to understand a text
Academic writing skills	Commas
Writing task	Write facts

UNL⌀CK YOUR KNOWLEDGE

Write the sports from the wordbox in the correct column of the table.
Use the glossary on page 197 to help you.

football   judo   karate   tennis

martial art	ball or team game

WATCH AND LISTEN

    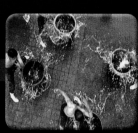

PREPARING TO WATCH

USING VISUALS TO PREDICT CONTENT

1 ▶ Watch the video. Circle the things you see.

> a busy city   a forest   pensioners   morning   tourists
> night   a teacher   young men in traditional clothes
> young men in modern clothes   an ancient painting

UNDERSTANDING KEY VOCABULARY

2 Match the opposites. Use a dictionary to help you.

1	mind	**a**	dangerous
2	fit	**b**	weak
3	slow	**c**	unfit
4	busy	**d**	body
5	strong	**e**	fast
6	safe	**f**	quiet

WHILE WATCHING

UNDERSTANDING MAIN IDEAS

3 ▶ Watch again. Circle the correct answer (a–c).

1 Why are sport and exercise popular in China?
   a because team games are popular
   b because health is important
   c because famous people do sport and exercise

2 Why are Tai-chi and Kung-fu popular in China?
   a because football is not popular
   b because people learn Tai-chi and Kung-fu at school
   c because Tai-chi and Kung-fu are part of Chinese culture and history

4 ▶ Watch again. Write words from Exercise 2 in the gaps (1–5).

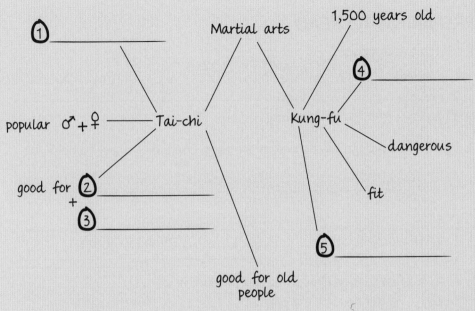

5 Match the people (1–4) below to a sport (a–d).

1 Sara is 22. She works in an office. She works
   many hours. She wants to be fit and healthy.
2 Dandan is 15. He is fit and healthy. He likes
   team games.
3 Jing Wei is 19. She wants to be fit and strong.
4 Andrew is 69. He wants to be healthy.

a Tai-chi
b Kung-fu
c Football
d Tennis

DISCUSSION

6 Work with a partner. Ask and answer the questions below.

1 Why do people do martial arts like Tai-chi?
2 Can you be fit and healthy and not do sport? How?

READING 1

PREPARING TO READ

UNDERSTANDING
KEY VOCABULARY

1 Match the opposites.

1	national	**a**	fast
2	exciting	**b**	local
3	slow	**c**	boring

2 Write the words from the box in the gaps. Use a dictionary to help you.

> player   billion   competitions   result   fan   million   questionnaire

1 A _____ has nine '0's – 1,000,000,000.
2 My favourite football _____ is Fernando Torres.
3 Every new student writes answers to the university _____ .
4 Ali is a fast runner. He comes first in running _____ .
5 Jolly loves tennis. She is a big _____ of the game.
6 A _____ has six '0's – 1,000,000.
7 The _____ of Liverpool's game is not very good – 7–0!

Using your knowledge

Use your knowledge of the world to ask questions before you read a text.
Questions can:
• give you a reason to read
• help you understand.

USING YOUR
KNOWLEDGE TO
PREDICT CONTENT

3 What are the top five favourite sports in the world? Write your ideas below.

1 _____
2 _____
3 _____
4 _____
5 _____

4 Work with a partner. Compare your answers to Exercise 3.

WHILE READING

READING FOR
MAIN IDEAS

5 Read the text. Match the sports in the box to the correct paragraphs (1–5).

> Field hockey   Motor racing   Cricket   Tennis   Football

THE WORLD'S TOP FIVE FAVOURITE SPORTS

We asked 1,379 people from 18 different countries: 'What is your favourite sport?'.

Here are the results of our questionnaire.

1 _____

This is the number one sport in the world. There are over 3.5 billion fans! Millions of children play football at school. It is also the most popular sport to watch. Over 700 million people watch the World Cup on television. The most popular national teams are Brazil, Argentina and Spain. The most popular local teams are Manchester United, Real Madrid and Chelsea.

2 _____

Yes! Many people are surprised but it is true. Some people think this English game is slow and boring. But many people think it is fast and exciting. It is very popular in India, Pakistan, Sri Lanka, Australia, New Zealand and England. 2.2 billion people watch the World Cup.

3 _____

Another surprise! The number 3 sport in the world is not basketball or baseball. Almost 2 billion people around the world watch and play field hockey. The best teams are from Germany, Australia and Korea.

4 _____

About 1 billion people in the world watch or play this game. The most popular competitions are the Australian Open, the French Open, Wimbledon and the US Open. Rafael Nadal from Spain and Maria Sharapova from Russia are famous players.

5 _____

Over 150 million people watch Formula 1 on television. Grand Prix races take place in over 18 countries, including Malaysia, Korea, Italy and the United Arab Emirates. Famous drivers include the Brazilian Ayrton Senna and Britain's Lewis Hamilton.

6 Read the text again. Write true (T) or false (F) next to the statements (1–8) below.

1 Brazil has a popular cricket team. _____
2 There is a famous Russian tennis player in the text. _____
3 Ayrton Senna was from Malaysia. _____
4 There are 2.2 billion football fans in the world. _____
5 The Australian Open is a tennis competition. _____
6 700 million people watch Formula 1. _____
7 Some people think cricket is slow. _____
8 Basketball is the number 3 sport in the world. _____

DISCUSSION

7 Work with a partner. Ask and answer the questions (1–3) below.

1 What other sports are popular?
2 What are the most popular sports in your country?
3 What is your favourite sport?

READING 2

PREPARING TO READ

1 Circle the three correct answers.

We use capital letters with ...

a nouns
b names of people
c the first word in a sentence
d names of sports
e names of places

2 Scan the text on the opposite page quickly. Find the names of six famous sportsmen from Brazil. Look for the capital letters to find the names.

3 Work with a partner. Do you know the sportsmen in the text?

4 Match the words (1–6) to the correct meanings (a–f).

1 In total   a all places
2 everywhere   b a place that gives information to people
3 everybody   c something you buy before you go on a train
4 a tourist office   d the whole amount
5 do something online   e all the people
6 ticket   f use the internet to do something

WHILE READING

5 Read the text. Write (F) for football, (C) for capoeira or (MR) for motor racing next to the statements below.

1 People play it on the beach.   _____
2 People do it in the park.   _____
3 You can watch it in São Paulo at Interlagos Speedway.   _____
4 People from other countries come to Brazil to learn this sport.   _____
5 Brazilians play this game in their free time.   _____

6 Write words from the text in the gaps.

One of the most (1) _____ sports in Brazil is football.
Many famous football (2) _____ come from Brazil.
Another popular sport is (3) _____ . You can see groups
of people training in the (4) _____ .
(5) _____ is also popular in Brazil. Many famous
motor-racing (6) _____ come from this country.

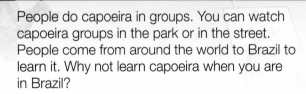

Sport in Brazil

Watch, play, learn!

Capoeira is a popular type of exercise.

Football is very important in Brazil. People play football everywhere, and everybody plays. Adults and children play football in their free time. They usually play on football fields, but sometimes they play football on the beach or in the street. Brazil has many world-famous footballers, like Pele, Kakà, and Ronaldinho. In total, there are over 13 million players and 29,208 football clubs. If you want to watch a football match, you can buy tickets from any tourist office.

Football is not the only popular sport in Brazil. Capoeira is an important part of Brazilian culture. It is a mix of martial arts, exercise and music.

People do capoeira in groups. You can watch capoeira groups in the park or in the street. People come from around the world to Brazil to learn it. Why not learn capoeira when you are in Brazil?

Motor racing is also popular. Piquet, Senna and Massa are famous Formula 1 drivers from Brazil. Many Brazilians like motor racing and watch it on television. In November, you can watch Formula 1 Grand Prix live in São Paulo at Interlagos Speedway. At other times of the year, you can watch Stock Car Brasil. You can buy tickets for motor-racing events online.

DISCUSSION

7 Work with a partner. Ask and answer the questions below.

1 What sports do people watch on TV in your country?
2 Is it better to watch sport live or on TV? Why?
3 Which of these activities are good ways to exercise?
   a horse riding
   b doing housework
   c walking
   d cooking
   e looking after children
   f shopping
   g swimming

UNL⌀CK READING AND WRITING SKILLS 1

◉ LANGUAGE DEVELOPMENT

EXPLANATION

Sports collocations

One type of *collocation* is a verb + a noun or noun phrase. Use the verbs *do, play* and *go* with nouns for sport and exercise.

Use *do* with martial arts and sport or exercise you do alone.

I do Kung-fu. We do exercise for one hour every morning.
Mei does karate.

Use *play* with team games and sports with a ball.

I play football. We play volleyball. Hiroshi plays baseball.

Use *go* with *-ing* nouns.

I go skiing. We go swimming. Faisal goes running.

1 Write the verbs from the box in the gaps. Use the glossary on page 197 to help you understand the words in bold.

UNLOCK ONLINE

~~do~~   plays (x2)   goes   play (x3)   go (x2)   do

1 Many children ___do___ **karate**.
2 We _____ **basketball** every Sunday.
3 Agata and Ursula _____ **jogging** on the beach.
4 Ginger _____ **squash** at lunch times.
5 Philip _____ **football** for the university team.
6 Children in Pakistan _____ **cricket** in their free time.
7 I _____ **exercise** three times a week.
8 People in my country _____ **baseball** at school.
9 Everybody _____ **swimming** in summer.
10 My family _____ **horse riding** every Sunday.

EXPLANATION

Prepositions

The words *in*, *on* and *at* are examples of *prepositions*. We use prepositions with particular nouns.

Adults and children play football in their free time.
They usually play on football fields, but sometimes they play football
on the beach or in the street.
People do capoeira in groups.
We watch football on television.
We have animals on our farm.

2 Write the prepositions *in* or *on* in the gaps.

1 Rugby is a popular sport _____ **Australia**.
2 You play rugby _____ **a field** called a 'pitch'.
3 Millions of fans watch the Rugby World Cup _____ **television**.
4 Fans can watch football or cricket _____ **a stadium**.
5 Children play tennis _____ **the street** in summer.
6 Iris goes horse riding _____ **a farm**.

3 Write the nouns in bold in Exercise 2 in the correct column below.

on + noun	*in* + noun

EXPLANATION

Adjectives

Adjectives describe qualities. Write adjectives:

- before a noun, e.g. good climate, popular sport, famous player.
- after *is/are (not)*, e.g. Football is exciting. Tennis is popular in my country. Cricket players are fast.

4 Write the adjectives in the box next to the correct opposites.

unknown   soft   boring   safe   unpopular   easy   cheap

hard	
exciting	
dangerous	
expensive	
difficult	
popular	
famous	

CRITICAL THINKING

At the end of this unit, you will write facts. Look at this unit's writing task in the box below.

Write facts about a popular sport in your country.

Ideas maps

An *ideas map* can help you remember new vocabulary and new information.

An ideas map of Reading 1 *The World's top five sports* is below.

1 Work with a partner. Create an ideas map of Reading 2 *Sport in Brazil: Watch, play, learn!*.

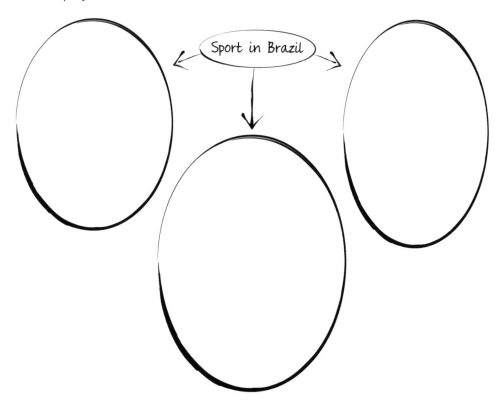

Sport in Brazil

2 Use the ideas map checklist to check your ideas map.

IDEAS MAP CHECKLIST	✔
Does your ideas map have three sports?	
Are there key words/numbers next to each sport?	
Do the names of people and places have capital letters?	
Can you use the ideas map to remember the main ideas of the text?	
Does your ideas map have different colours?	

3 Look at the ideas maps of other students in the class.

WRITING

GRAMMAR FOR WRITING

EXPLANATION

Subject – Verb – Adjective

A sentence is about a *subject*. The subject is a pronoun, a noun or a noun phrase. Write the *verb* after the *subject* in a sentence. Write a noun, a noun phrase or an adjective after the verb *am/is/are (not)*.

> Noun or noun phrase: My father is a doctor. My sister is a serious student.
> Adjective: Television is boring. Football is exciting. Kung-fu is dangerous.

1 Circle the option that is true for you or your country.

UNLOCK ONLINE

1 I *am / am not* a big fan of sports.
2 Kung-fu *is / is not* popular in my country.
3 I think football is *exciting / boring*.
4 I think motor racing is *safe / dangerous*.
5 Tickets for football are *cheap / expensive* in my country.
6 It is *easy / difficult* to buy tickets for football in my country.
7 Horse riding *is / is not* expensive in my country.

2 Put the words in order to make a sentence.

1 is / . / in / Russia / Ice hockey / popular

_____

2 Japan / in / . / a / baseball player / is / Minoru Iwata / famous

_____

3 not / . / popular / is / Basketball / country / in / my

_____

4 cheap / are / Tickets / for football / .

_____

5 . / It / tickets / buy / for tennis / to / difficult / is

_____

EXPLANATION

Subject – Verb – Adverb

Adverbs can say when (time) or where (place) something happens. Prepositional phrases can be an adverb.

> time: Faisal plays tennis on Wednesday. Rabea goes swimming in the evening.
> place: Children play football in the street. I go running in the park.

3 Underline the prepositional phrases in the sentences below.

1 I play tennis on Monday and Wednesday. _____
2 In summer, we go horse riding. _____
3 I watch Arsenal football club in the stadium. _____
4 Children go ice skating on the lake. _____
5 Many people play volleyball on the beach. _____
6 I do judo on Sunday evening. _____
7 In winter, we go skiing. _____
8 Ahmed goes surfing in the morning. _____

4 Write (T) for time or (P) for place next to the prepositional phrases in Exercise 3.

5 Correct the sentences.

1 People play tennis on the park.

_____

2 Football games are in Wednesday evening.

_____

3 Children play football in the beach.

_____

4 On spring, we play baseball.

_____

5 I do exercise in Monday.

_____

ACADEMIC WRITING SKILLS

EXPLANATION

Commas

Write commas (,) in a sentence. Commas separate parts of a sentence or things in a list. Use a comma:

- after a prepositional phrase at the beginning of a sentence
- between two nouns in a list.

In summer, we go swimming. In the evenings, I watch TV.
Faisal plays football, tennis, basketball and baseball. He goes to the gym on Monday, Wednesday, Thursday and Saturday.

1 Correct the punctuation in the sentences. (1–5). Add capital letters, commas and full stops.

1 ayrton senna was a famous driver from brazil

_____

2 in winter the children go ice skating

_____

3 in summer we go swimming in the river

_____

4 in may june july and august we play baseball

_____

5 john does karate in the park

_____

SPELLING

2 Put the letters in the correct order to make the names of sports. Use the glossary on page 197 to help you.

1 oftoblal   f_____
2 sekbatallb   b_____
3 insnte   t_____
4 yehcko   h_____
5 selbalba   b_____

3 Put the letters in the correct order to make the names of countries.

1 ketury   T_____
2 landaiht   T_____
3 inach   C_____
4 pajan   J_____
5 razibl   B_____
6 ilehc   C_____
7 ostuh okera   S_____ K_____
8 edtinu baar irmetsae   U_____ A_____ E_____

PLAN

WRITE A FIRST
DRAFT

EDIT

WRITING TASK

Write facts about a popular sport in your country.

1 Look at the examples of ideas maps in the Critical thinking section. Make an ideas map for a popular sport in your country.

2 Write answers that are true for you in the gaps.

_____ (name of sport) is very popular in

_____ (your country).

3 Write sentences that are true for your sport.

1 Write a sentence about the people that like the sport (e.g. young people, old people, men, women).

2 Write a sentence about the places people do the sport (e.g. in a stadium, in a park, on the beach).

3 Write a sentence about the times people do the sport (e.g. in summer, in winter, in July).

4 Write a sentence about famous sportsmen or women in your sport.

5 Write a sentence about the number of fans for your sport.

6 Write a sentence about the places you can see your sport.

7 Write a sentence about the price of tickets for your sport (e.g. expensive, cheap).

4 Use the task checklist to review your sentences.

TASK CHECKLIST	✔
Do your sentences describe a popular sport in my country?	
Does every sentence have a subject and a verb?	
Is there an adjective, a noun or a noun phrase after the verb am/is/are?	
Do names of people and countries begin with a capital letter?	
Is there a comma after a prepositional phrase for time at the beginning of a sentence?	

5 Make any necessary changes to your sentences.

OBJECTIVES REVIEW

6 Check your objectives.

I can ...

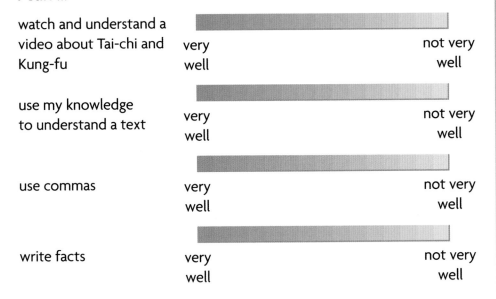

watch and understand a video about Tai-chi and Kung-fu

very well not very well

use my knowledge to understand a text

very well not very well

use commas

very well not very well

write facts

very well not very well

WORDLIST

UNIT VOCABULARY		
baseball (n)	famous (adj)	national (adj)
basketball (n)	fan (n)	online (adj)
boring (adj)	horse riding (n)	player (n)
cheap (adj)	ice skating (n)	rugby (n)
competition (n)	jogging (n)	squash (n)
exciting (adj)	judo (n)	team game (n)
exercise (n)	karate (n)	tennis (n)
expensive (adj)	martial art (n)	ticket (n)

LEARNING OBJECTIVES

Watch and listen	Watch and understand a video about the *dabbawallas* of Mumbai
Reading skills	Read a text for detail
Academic writing skills	Use contractions
Writing task	Write sentences

UNL⊘CK YOUR KNOWLEDGE

Read the sentences (1–5) below and write the jobs from the box in the gaps. Use a dictionary to help you.

architect   manager   software engineer
nurse   primary school teacher

1 A _____ manages people.
2 An _____ designs buildings.
3 A _____ looks after people in
   a hospital.
4 A _____ manages software.
5 A _____ teaches young children.

WATCH AND LISTEN

PREPARING TO WATCH

UNDERSTANDING KEY VOCABULARY

1 Write the words in the gaps. Use the glossary on page 198 to help you.

> symbol   cook   deliver   lunch   kitchen   paint

1 My brother is a _____ . He makes good food.
2 Children _____ pictures of houses, their mother and their father.
3 I have _____ at 2 pm. I eat with my family.
4 Postmen _____ letters to houses and offices.
5 This is an example of a _____ : ♥
6 There are five rooms in my house. This room is my _____ .

WHILE WATCHING

UNDERSTANDING MAIN IDEAS

2 ▶ Watch the video about the 'dabbawallas' of Mumbai and circle the correct options (a–c).

1 Mumbai is
  a a busy city.
  b a quiet city.
  c a small city.
2 Dabbawallas deliver lunch
  a to schools.
  b to offices.
  c to homes.
3 Dabbawallas deliver food by
  a train and bicycle.
  b bicycle only.
  c car and motorbike.

3  Watch again and circle the correct words in the notes below.

Video – Dabbawallas
- In Mumbai – 200,000 (1) dabbawallas / workers
- (2) Cooks / Dabbawallas put lunches in tiffin tins
- Tiffin tins → (3) bus / train station
- Dabbawallas (4) write names / paint symbols on tiffin tins
- (5) 4,000 / 5,000 dabbawallas in Mumbai

DISCUSSION

4 Work with a partner. Ask and answer the questions below.

1 Is the dabbawallas' job easy or difficult?
2 Do people deliver food to offices and homes in your country? What kind of food do they deliver?

READING 1

PREPARING TO READ

PREVIEWING

1 Look at the texts. Where are they from? Circle the correct answer (a–c).

a a website for tourists   c a website for food and drink
b a website for jobs

UNDERSTANDING
KEY VOCABULARY

2 Match the sentences. Use a dictionary to help you understand the words in bold.

1 My mother teaches at a university.   a His **salary** is $120,000 a year.
2 Faisal is an **employer**.   b She has a lot of **experience**.
3 My sister is a good software engineer.   c She **trains** teachers.
4 Pankaj is an architect in Los Angeles.   d His company has 200 workers.

3 Read the sentences (1–6) below and write the words from the box in the gaps. Use the glossary on page 198 to help you.

> full-time   fit   part-time   healthy   friendly   fluent

1 Fruit is _____ .
2 Daria runs every morning. She is very _____ .
3 Meryem speaks _____ Turkish and English.
4 I have a _____ job. I work two hours after school.
5 Osman is a popular student – he is very _____ .
6 I have a _____ job. I work from Monday to Friday.

WHILE READING

SCANNING TO
FIND INFORMATION

4 Scan the texts. Write words from the texts in the gaps.

	text A	text B	text C
1 What is the job?	(1) _____	pilot	(2) _____
2 Which country is the job in?	(3) _____	(4) _____	Japan
3 Who is the employer?	Renji Hospital	(5) _____	Kitahiroshima Primary School
4 What is the salary?	CNY16,800 per month	(6) _____	(7) _____
5 Is the job full-time (FT) or part-time (PT)?	FT	PT	(8) _____

Find_my_job.com

A

YOUR SEARCH

AREA(S): Medicine

JOB(S): Nurse

✉ Email me jobs like this

RSS Feeds

LOCATION ▼ China

SALARY FROM ▼ Any

SALARY TO ▼ Any

Renji Hospital

Renji Hospital is part of Shanghai Jiao Tong University School of Medicine. We train and teach doctors and nurses.

We are looking for a nurse to work at the hospital and train student nurses. You have to work early mornings and late nights.

Applicants must have 10 years' experience. They must also speak fluent Chinese and English.

SALARY: CNY 16,800 per month

TYPE: Full-time (including weekends)

B

YOUR SEARCH

AREA(S): Aviation

JOB(S): Pilot

✉ Email me jobs like this

RSS Feeds

LOCATION ▼ India

SALARY FROM ▼ Any

SALARY TO ▼ Any

FlyHigh air transport company

FlyHigh is a small company in Mumbai. We provide private air transport in Asia.

We are looking for a pilot. All our pilots are friendly and speak English, Hindi and Urdu.

Applicants must have 2 years' experience. You have to work weekends. You must be fit and healthy.

SALARY: INR 200,000 per journey

TYPE: Part-time

C

YOUR SEARCH

AREA(S): Education

JOB(S): Teacher

✉ Email me jobs like this

RSS Feeds

LOCATION ▼ Japan

SALARY FROM ▼ Any

SALARY TO ▼ Any

Kitahiroshima Primary School

Kitahiroshima is a private English school. Our staff are friendly and interested in teaching children.

We are looking for a Maths teacher to teach grades 1–3.

Applicants must have a university education. They must speak English.

SALARY: JPY 320,000 per month

TYPE: Full-time

> ## Reading for detail
>
> *Reading for detail* means checking that you understand a text. One way of checking for detail is to follow the steps below:
>
> - Ask a question (e.g. *Renji Hospital trains nurses – is this true or false?*)
> - Scan the text to find key words and sentences (e.g. *Renji, train, nurses, doctors*)
> - Read that sentence to find the correct answer: (e.g. *We train and teach doctors and nurses.*)

READING FOR DETAIL

 UNL♥CK ONLINE

5 Read the texts again. Write true (T) or false (F) next to the statements (1–6) below.

1 The pilot at *FlyHigh* must speak three languages. ____
2 The teacher at Kitahiroshima Primary School has to teach grade 12. ____
3 The nurse at Renji Hospital must have 10 years' experience. ____
4 Teachers at Kitahiroshima Primary School are friendly. ____
5 Pilots at *FlyHigh* have to work nights. ____
6 The nurse at Renji Hospital must speak two languages. ____

READING BETWEEN THE LINES

WORKING OUT MEANING FROM CONTEXT

6 Read the texts again and underline the words from the box below.

> location   applicant   education   medicine

7 Read the definitions (1–4) below and write the words from the box in Exercise 6 in the gaps.

1 _____ : a science that doctors and nurses study
2 _____ : teaching and learning
3 _____ : a place
4 _____ : a person that wants a job

DISCUSSION

8 Work with a partner. Ask and answer the questions below.

1 What jobs do people in your family do?
2 Do you have a job? Why / Why not?
3 Where can you find information about jobs?
4 Which jobs are the most difficult? Why?

READING 2

PREPARING TO READ

1 Read the sentences (1–7) below and write the words and phrases from the box in the gaps. Use a dictionary to help you.

> soon   fitness instructor   great   apply
> long hours   gym   link

1 *Tetris* is a _____ computer game. I play it every day.
2 This is an example of a _____ : www.cambridge.org
3 You are going to read three texts _____ .
4 Thousands of people _____ for a job with Google every day.
5 Yunis is a _____ in Liverpool. He teaches people exercise.
6 Doctors and nurses work _____ . They start work early and they finish late.
7 Phuong likes doing exercise. She goes to the _____ every morning.

WHILE READING

2 Scan the texts on the next page. Write the correct jobs in the gaps.

1 The email to Çağ is about a job as a _____ .
2 The email to Erik is about a job as a _____ .
3 The email to Daria is about a job as a _____ .

3 Scan the texts again. Write the correct city or town in the gaps.

1 The job for Çağ is in _____ .
2 The job for Erik is in _____ .
3 The job for Daria is in _____ .

4 Scan the texts again. Write the correct number(s) in the gaps.

1 Daria must teach grades _____ to _____ .
2 There are _____ students in a fitness class at the gym.
3 The salary for Erik's job is £ _____ per month.

5 Read the texts again. Write (C) for Çağ, (E) for Erik or (D) for Daria next to the statements (1–5) below.

1 He/She must be good with people.   _____
2 He/She has to be fluent in three languages. _____
3 He/She must have two years' experience.   _____
4 He/She has to get up early.   _____
5 He/She must work long hours.   _____

A

To: c_evgin@gmail.com
From: k_t_b1001@yahoo.com
Subject: Interesting job for you!

Çağ!

I have found a great job for you. It's for a full-time fitness instructor. The job is at David Allen's Irish Gym in Manchester.

You have to get up early in the morning. There are 12 students in each group. You have to be very friendly and good with people. The wages are very good – they pay £28 an hour. You don't have to work on Friday or Saturday.

I think you'll like this job. Here's the link: www.ukjobs.co.uk/Fitness-instructor

Apply soon!

Karel

B

To: erik1221@yahoo.com
From: ingrid_soljberg@hotmail.com
Subject: IT'S MOM – LOOK AT THIS JOB!

Erik,

I have found a great job for you. It's in Oslo – here's the link: www.itcompany.org/jobs
I know this company.

The job is for a software engineer. It's full-time. They pay £4,150 per month!

You must have a university degree (in computer science!) and you have to have 2 years' experience. It also says that you must speak Norwegian. You don't have to speak fluent Norwegian – so it's OK for you.

Please apply soon!

Love,

Mom x

C

To: akhrorova_dasha@hotmail.com
From: olly_murgatroyd@gmail.com
Subject: Do you want a job in a great country?

Dear Daria,

I hope you're well. I have a great job for you. I think you'll like it – it's in South Korea! I know you love Korean movies, especially movies with Cha Tae-hyun.

The job is in Yeonggwang. It's a small town in the south of the country.

The job is at a high school. You have to teach English and French to grades 10 to 12. You speak fluent English and French (and Russian!)
You don't have to speak Korean so this is a great job for you. You have to work long hours. But you are a very serious teacher. I know you work hard.

Here's the link: www.skoreajobs.com/Education/HS/Languages

Good luck!

Oliver

DISCUSSION

6 Work with a partner. Ask and answer the questions below.

1 What jobs are popular with young people in your country?
2 What job(s) would you like to do?
3 What job(s) would you not like to do?

◉ LANGUAGE DEVELOPMENT

VOCABULARY FOR JOBS

1 Make sentences about jobs. Write the verb phrases from the box in the correct places in column B of the table.

> prepares food   builds houses   makes movies
> looks after animals   looks after money   gives people medicine
> looks after passengers   puts out fires   manages people

A jobs	B activities	C locations
1 A vet		
2 A manager		
3 A doctor		
4 A builder		in towns and cities.
5 An accountant		in a company.
6 A chef		
7 A fireman		in towns and cities.
8 A flight attendant		
9 An actor	plays a character	
10 A film director		in different countries.

2 Write the prepositional phrases from the box in the correct places in column C of the table. Remember to write the full stop.

> in hospital.   in a movie.   in farms and zoos.
> in an office.   in a restaurant.   on a plane.

Adjective phrases

An *adjective phrase* describes the subject of the sentence. The adjective phrase is after **a form of the verb** *to be*.

One type of adjective phrase is *very* + an adjective.

Pilots have to be **very intelligent**. Nurses must be **very kind**.

Another type of adjective phrase is an adjective + *and* + an adjective.

Pilots must be **fit and healthy**. Nurses have to be **kind and helpful**.

Another type of adjective phrase is *good at* + a noun or *good with* + a noun.

Pilots have to be **good at Maths**. Nurses must be **good with people**.

3 Read the sentences (1–10) and circle the best words and phrases.

1 A fireman has to be *smart / fit and strong*.
2 A primary school teacher has to be *good with food / kind and patient*.
3 A fireman doesn't have to be *good with people / fit and healthy*.
4 A doctor must be *very intelligent / very fit and strong*.
5 A nurse doesn't have to be *good with computers / good with people*.
6 A software engineer has to be *good at Maths / kind and patient*.
7 A flight attendant has to be *polite and friendly / creative*.
8 A film director must be very *creative / polite and friendly*.
9 An actor doesn't have to be *beautiful / creative*.
10 A chef has to be *good with food / smart*.

CRITICAL THINKING

At the end of this unit, you will write sentences. Look at this unit's writing task in the box below.

> Write a description of a job for a friend.

Questionnaires

A *questionnaire* is a list of questions. We use questionnaires to discover new information.

One kind of questionnaire is a *Likert scale*. In a Likert scale, you read a statement then circle the answer that is true for you.

1 Read the statements and circle the answer that is true for you.

1 = strongly disagree
2 = disagree
3 = neither agree nor disagree
4 = agree
5 = strongly agree

1 I am very healthy.
  1   2   3   4   5

2 I am fit and strong.
  1   2   3   4   5

3 I am good with people.
  1   2   3   4   5

4 I am very patient.
  1   2   3   4   5

5 I am kind and helpful.
  1   2   3   4   5

6 I am good with children.
  1   2   3   4   5

7 I am very smart.
  1   2   3   4   5

8 I am good at Maths.
  1   2   3   4   5

9 I am very creative.
  1   2   3   4   5

10 I am good with computers.
  1   2   3   4   5

11 I am good with animals.
  1   2   3   4   5

12 I am good at foreign languages.
  1   2   3   4   5

2 Work with a partner. Read your partner's answers to the questionnaire. Choose the best job for your partner from the box below.

manager   software engineer   doctor   teacher
actor   fitness instructor   vet

WRITING

GRAMMAR FOR WRITING

must and have to

We can use *must* + infinitive or *have to* + infinitive to say that something is necessary.

> Doctors **must be** intelligent. Doctors **have to** be intelligent. Doctors **must have** a good education. Doctors **have to have** a good education.

We use *must* + infinitive for *I, you, he, she, it, we* and *they*. We never use *must to* + infinitive.

> A nurse must to be kind and helpful. → A nurse **must be** kind and helpful.

We use *have to* + infinitive for *I, you, we* and *they*.

> Managers **have to** be good with people. They **have to** be good with people.

We use *has to* + infinitive for *he, she* and *it*.

> A manager **has to** be good with people. He **has to** be good with people.

UNL**O**CK
ONLINE

1 Correct the mistakes in the sentences (1–8) below.

1 A builder musts be strong and healthy.
2 Fireman have work long hours.
3 A manager have to be helpful.
4 Teachers must patient.
5 A software engineer must to be good at Maths.
6 Vets have good with animals.
7 An architect must to creative.
8 An actor must to play a character in a movie.

have to

We can use *do not have to / does not have to* + infinitive to say that something is not necessary.

We use *do not have to* + infinitive for *I, you, we* and *they*.

> Actors **do not have to** be good with computers.

We use *does not have to* + infinitive for *he, she* and *it*.

> A film director **does not have to** be good at Maths.

We do <u>not</u> use *must not* + infinitive to say that something is not necessary.

2 Put the words in order to make sentences.

1 does / have / houses / build / to / An / not / architect / .

_____

2 and / manager / to / A / not / does / be / patient / kind / have / .

_____

3 computers / have / be / not / do / with / Nurses / to / good / .

_____

4 smart / be / Actors / not / have / do / to / .

_____

5 A / teacher / French / have / good / Maths / be / at / not / does / to / .

_____

6 strong / doctor / A / does / have / be / to / not / .

_____

Joining sentences with *and*

A sentence always has a subject and a verb. We use *and* to join two sentences that have the same subject and verb. We do not have to repeat the subject and verb if it is the same in both sentences.

Sentences 1 and 2:

You have to be very friendly. You have to be good with people.

Join sentences 1 and 2 with *and*:

You have to be very friendly **and** you have to be good with people.

Do not repeat the same subject and verb:

You have to be very friendly and ~~you have to be~~ good with people.

New sentence:

You have to be very friendly **and** good with people.

3 Join each pair of sentences (1–4) below to make one sentence with *and*.

1 Applicants must be smart. Applicants must be polite.

_____

2 You do not have to be fit. You do not have to be strong.

_____

3 Firemen have to be fit. Firemen have to be healthy.

_____

4 Daria has to teach English. Daria has to teach French.

_____

ACADEMIC WRITING SKILLS

PUNCTUATION

Contractions

We can join two words with an *apostrophe* ('). The joined word is called a *contraction*.

I am a doctor. → I'm a doctor.
Philip is an engineer. → Philip's an engineer.
They are architects. → They're architects.

One kind of contraction is *do not* → *don't* and *does not* → *doesn't*.

You do not have to be good at Maths. → You **don't** have to be good at Maths.
She does not have to be strong. → She **doesn't** have to be strong.

We do not usually use contractions in academic writing. We can use contractions in emails to friends.

Rewrite the sentences below (1–5) with no contractions.

1 I'm very happy.

_____

2 Daria's a serious teacher.

_____

3 Hamdan's a good friend.

_____

4 I hope you're well.

_____

5 You don't have to work on Friday.

_____

UNLOCK READING AND WRITING SKILLS 1

WRITING TASK

Write a description of a job for a friend.

1 Look at your partner's answers to the questionnaire in the Critical Thinking section. Write information about a job for your partner in the email below.

WRITE A FIRST
DRAFT

To:
From:
Subject:

Dear _____ *(write your partner's name),*

I hope you're well. I have a great job for you. I think you'll like it – it's in
_____ *(write the name of country)!*

The job is in _____ *(write the name of the
city/town).* It _____

_____

(write a sentence to describe the city).

The job is for a _____ *(write the name of
the job).* It's _____ *(write _full-time_ or _part-time_).* The salary
is _____ *(write the salary)* per month.

_____

_____

_____

_____

_____

_____

*(Write sentences about the job. Use _must_ and _have to_ with
adjective phrases.)*

Here's the link: www.discoverjobs4you.com

Good luck!

_____ *(write your name)*

2 Use the task checklist to review your sentences.

TASK CHECKLIST	✔
Do your sentences use *must* and *have to* to say that something is necessary?	
Do your sentences use *do / does not have to* to say that something is not necessary?	
Do your sentences use adjective phrases to describe a job applicant?	
Do your sentences use contractions?	

3 Make any necessary changes to your sentences.

OBJECTIVES REVIEW

4 Check your objectives.

I can ...

watch and understand
a video about the   very   not very
dabbawallas of Mumbai   well   well

read a text for detail   very   not very
                                 well   well

use contractions   very   not very
                                 well   well

write sentences   very   not very
                                 well   well

WORDLIST

UNIT VOCABULARY		
bicycle (n)	healthy (adj)	medicine (n)
building (n)	hospital (n)	nurse (n)
cook (n)	kitchen (n)	paint (v)
friendly (adj)	lunch (n)	software (n)
great (adj)	manager (n)	soon (adv)

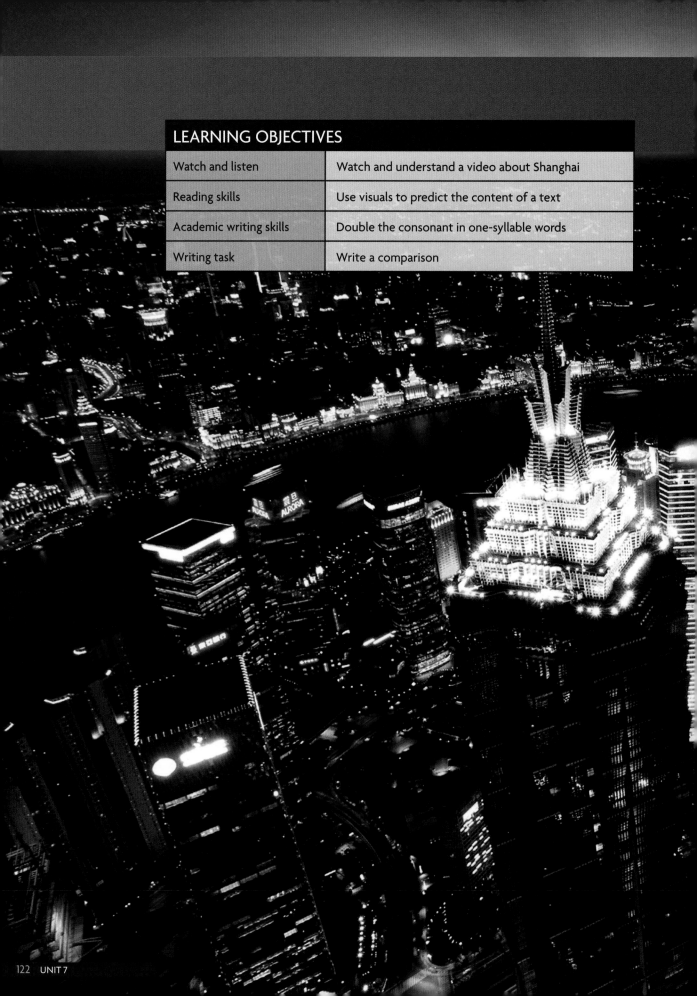

LEARNING OBJECTIVES

Watch and listen	Watch and understand a video about Shanghai
Reading skills	Use visuals to predict the content of a text
Academic writing skills	Double the consonant in one-syllable words
Writing task	Write a comparison

HOMES AND BUILDINGS | UNIT 7

UNL⊘CK YOUR KNOWLEDGE

Work with a partner. Ask and answer the questions below.

1 Do you live in a house or an apartment?
2 Do you like tall buildings? Why / Why not?
3 Are there any tall buildings in your city?

PREPARING TO WATCH

USING YOUR KNOWLEDGE TO PREDICT CONTENT

1 You are going to watch a video about Shanghai. Before you watch, circle the correct options (a–c).

1 Shanghai is
   a the capital city of China.
   b a busy city in China.
   c a big city in Vietnam.

2 Today, the population of Shanghai is
   a 8 million.
   b 14 million.
   c 23 million.

3 The population of Shanghai today is
   a smaller than in 1990.
   b the same as in 1990.
   c bigger than in 1990.

4 Today, Shanghai needs more
   a homes.
   b offices.
   c jobs.

2 Check the meanings of the words in the table below. Use the glossary on page 198 to help you.

	A see	B hear
swimming pool		
restaurants		
shopping mall		
traffic		
park		
offices		
leisure centre		
shop		
lights		
apartments		

3 ▶ Watch the video with no sound. Put a tick (✓) next to things you <u>see</u> in column A in the table.

WHILE WATCHING

4 ▶ Watch the video with sound. Check your answers to Exercise 1.

5 ▶ Watch again. Put a tick (✓) next to things you <u>hear</u> in column B.

DISCUSSION

6 Work with a partner. Ask and answer the questions below.

1 Is your city bigger or smaller than Shanghai?
2 Is your city busier or quieter than Shanghai?
3 Is there a shopping mall or leisure centre near your home?

READING 1

PREPARING TO READ

UNDERSTANDING KEY VOCABULARY

1 Write the words from the box in the correct places in the table below. Use the glossary on page 198 to help you. For some words, more than one answer is possible.

> roof   tall   glass   plastic   narrow   garden   ceiling
> wall   window   metal   room   mirror

things inside a house	things outside a house	adjectives to describe a house	materials

Using visuals to predict content

Visuals can be photographs, pictures, graphs or tables. Newspapers and magazines have a lot of photographs. You can use the photographs to help you understand the topic of the text.

USING VISUALS TO PREDICT CONTENT

2 Circle the phrases (a–d) to make statements you agree with.

I think the buildings in the photos are

a creative.

b not expensive.

c environmentally friendly.

d in the same city.

WHILE READING

SCANNING TO FIND INFORMATION

3 Read the text and tick the boxes in the table below.

	windows are different shapes	has glass walls	has a small garden on the roof	rooms are narrow
Japanese steep roof house				
Vietnamese 'garden home'				

Architect's World

EXPERT INTERVIEW

Professor Michael Chan teaches design to young architects at London School of Architecture. He has been at the school for 30 years. There have been many changes in home design in the last 30 years. This week, Michael Chan tells us more about new home design around the world.

Architect's World: What are your favourite home designs?

Michael Chan: I like Japanese designs. Many people in Japan build houses with unusual shapes. For example, the steep roof house (*see photo above*). This house is very tall and has a steep roof. The windows on the roof are different shapes and sizes. Inside the house, the rooms are very narrow and the ceilings are very high. It is simple and very small inside.

AW: What do you think about 'green' homes?

MC: It is very important to build houses that are environmentally friendly. My favourite green house is in Saigon, Vietnam. It is a 'garden home' (*see photo centre above*). This house is in the middle of a busy city but there are plants everywhere. From the street, people see a tall garden. But in fact it is a house. There are plants and trees in front of the glass walls. There is also a small garden on top of the roof. You can put chairs and a table there and enjoy tea with your family.

AW: What are popular building materials?

MC: Wood is very popular. It keeps your house warm in winter. Many architects use wood, metal and glass. Sometimes they use unusual building materials. For example, one architect from Amsterdam put mirrors on every wall of the house (*see photo above*). Other architects design houses with glass or even plastic walls.

4 Read the interview again. Write true (T) or false (F) next to the statements (1–6) below.

1 Professor Chan's favourite home designs are Korean. ___
2 Steep roof houses are small and narrow inside. ___
3 Professor Chan says it is important to build more homes in Vietnam. ___
4 The 'garden home' is in the centre of a big city. ___
5 Wood is more popular than plastic. ___
6 In Amsterdam, many architects put mirrors on the walls. ___

READING FOR DETAIL

UNLOCK ONLINE

PREPARING TO READ

1 Look at the text and the picture. Read the sentences (1–3) below and circle the correct words.

1 The text is from a/an *dictionary / encyclopedia*.
2 'Skyscraper' is a word for a *famous actor / tall building*.
3 The text has facts for *tourists / students*.

2 Read the sentences (1–5) below and write the words from the box in the gaps. Use the glossary on page 198 to help you.

> world-famous   open   modern   floor   lift

1 The shops _____ at 8 am in the morning.
2 Some _____ buildings are very unusual.
3 There is a nice restaurant on the second _____ .
4 You can take a _____ to the top of the building.
5 The Eiffel Tower is _____ .

WHILE READING

3 Scan the text. Write words from the text in the gaps in the table below.

	Shanghai World Financial Center	Taipei 101	Burj Khalifa
city	Shanghai	Taipei	(1) _____
height (m)	(2) _____	(3) _____	829
year	2008	2004	2010
number of floors	(4) _____	101	163
number of lifts	(5) _____	61	57
cost (USD)	850,000,000	(6) _____	1,500,000,000

Skyscrapers

What are skyscrapers?

Skyscrapers are very tall buildings. They are usually more than 300 metres tall.
You can see skyscrapers in cities around the world. Many countries build skyscrapers
to attract tourists. There are many skyscrapers in Asia, the Gulf, America and Europe.
Inside a skyscraper, there are offices, shops, restaurants and apartments.

What are some famous skyscrapers?

The Empire State Building in New York is a world-famous skyscraper. It has two million visitors
every year. It is popular with tourists but there are taller and more modern skyscrapers in the
Gulf and in Asia. The Shanghai World Financial Center, Taipei 101 and the Burj Khalifa in Dubai,
are taller than the Empire State Building. The Burj Khalifa is taller than the World Financial Center
and Taipei 101. Taipei 101 is taller than the World Financial Center.
The Burj Khalifa is also more modern than the other two buildings. It opened in 2010.

How much money do skyscrapers cost?

Skyscrapers are very expensive. They cost more money than other buildings.
The Burj Khalifa cost $1,500,000,000 to build. It was more expensive than the
World Financial Center ($850,000,000) but it was cheaper than Taipei 101.
Taipei 101 cost $1,760,000,000.

What is inside a skyscraper?

The Burj Khalifa has 163 floors.
This is more than Taipei 101 or the
World Financial Center. They have
101 floors each. All skyscrapers
have lifts. Taipei 101 has more lifts
than the Burj Khalifa or the World
Financial Center. It has 61 lifts.
The Burj Khalifa has 57 lifts but
the World Financial Center has
only 31. Many skyscrapers also
have shopping centres or malls
inside them. A lot of people come
shopping every day.

Shanghai World
Financial Center
(2008) **492 m**

Taipei 101
(2004) **509 m**

Burj Khalifa
(2010) **829 m**

Pronouns

You can match *pronouns* to nouns to help you understand a text.

> Skyscrapers are very tall buildings. **They** [*They* = Skyscrapers] are usually more than 300 m tall.
> The Empire State Building in New York is a world-famous skyscraper. **It** [*It* = The Empire State Building] has two million visitors every year.

UNDERSTANDING DISCOURSE

4 Match the buildings in the box to the pronouns in bold in the sentences (1–4) below.

> Shanghai World Financial Center   Taipei 101   Burj Khalifa

1 **It** was more expensive than the Shanghai World Financial Center ($850,000,000) or the Burj Khalifa ($1,500,000,000).
2 **It** opened in 2010.
3 **They** have 101 floors each.
4 **It** has 61 lifts.

◉ LANGUAGE DEVELOPMENT

VOCABULARY FOR BUILDINGS

1 Read the sentences (1–8) below and write the words from the box in the gaps.

> cinema   ice rink   Library   museum   Hotel
> mall   Stadium   train station

1 There are over 140 different shops in the Al Wahda _____ in Abu Dhabi.
2 In Wembley _____ in London, 90,000 fans can watch football.
3 The Izmailovo _____ in Moscow has 2,000 rooms you can stay in.
4 You can watch 3D movies at the _____ in the Westfield shopping centre in London.
5 More trains and passengers go to the Gare du Nord _____ in Paris than to King's Cross station in London.
6 You can see many treasures and famous paintings at the Louvre _____ in Paris.
7 In winter, you can skate at the _____ outside the Rockefeller Center in New York.
8 There are over 30,000,000 books in the National _____ of China.

The Rockefeller Center, New York

VOCABULARY FOR PARTS OF BUILDINGS

2 Read the sentences (1–5) and circle the correct words. Use a dictionary to help you.

1 You can leave your car in the *garden / car park*.
2 You can ride on the *escalator / stairs* to the next floor.
3 You go into a building through the *entrance / exit*.
4 You can walk up the *escalator / stairs* to the next floor.
5 You must go to the *entrance / exit* to get out if there is a fire.

ADJECTIVES

3 Match the adjectives (1–6) to their opposites (a–f).

1 big   a ugly
2 wide   b cheap
3 traditional   c narrow
4 old   d small
5 expensive   e modern
6 beautiful   f new

CRITICAL THINKING

At the end of this unit, you will write a comparison. Look at this unit's writing task in the box below.

> Write a comparison of two buildings.

Comparison of data

Data are facts or information about something. Data are often numbers. If we compare the facts or information about two or more things, we make a comparison of data.

UNDERSTAND

1 Read the data in Table 7.1 below. Write the words from the box in the gaps (1–3).

size   year   location

Table 7.1: Comparison of shopping malls

name	Country Club Plaza	Metro Centre	Istanbul Cevahir	SM Mall of Asia
country	USA	UK	Turkey	The Philippines
(1) _____	Kansas City	Gateshead	Istanbul	Manila
(2) _____	1922	1986	2005	2006
(3) _____	223,000m²	194,100m²	420,000m²	407,101m²
number of floors	1	2	6	6
number of shops	92	340	343	780
number of restaurants	48	25	48	300
number of cinemas	12	12	12	11

2 Work with a partner. Choose two shopping malls from Table 7.1. Ask and answer the questions (1–8). Write your answers on the lines below.

1 Which mall is more modern?

_____

_____

2 Which mall is older?

_____

_____

3 Which mall is bigger?

_____

_____

4 Which mall is smaller?

_____

_____

5 Which mall is taller?

_____

_____

6 Which mall has more shops?

_____

_____

7 Which mall has more restaurants?

_____

_____

8 Which mall has more cinemas?

_____

_____

WRITING

GRAMMAR FOR WRITING

EXPLANATION

Comparing quantities

We can compare quantities with *more* + a noun or a noun phrase + *than*. This phrase comes after the subject and the verb.

Taipei 101 has **more lifts than** the Shanghai World Financial Center.
Skyscrapers cost **more money than** other buildings.
The Izmailovo Hotel in Moscow has **more rooms than** the Hilton
New York.

1 Put the words and phrases in order to make sentences.

1 The Burj Khalifa / more / floors / Taipei 101 / has / than / .

_____

_____

2 visitors / than / has / The Louvre museum / the British Museum / more / .

_____

_____

3 more / than / The Istanbul Cevahir / the SM Mall of Asia / has / cinemas / .

_____

_____

4 has / The SM Mall of Asia / restaurants / than / more / the Metro Centre / .

_____

_____

5 shops / has / The Metro Centre / than / the Country Club Plaza / more / .

_____

_____

EXPLANATION

Comparative adjectives

Adjectives have three forms when we make comparisons. We use *syllables* to choose the correct form. A syllable is a word or part of a word with one vowel sound.

Adjectives with one or two syllables: *small, old, wide, narrow, quiet*
We add *-(e)r* + *than*.

> It is smaller **than** Taipei 101. It is older **than** the Metro Centre. It is wider **than** a typical Japanese house. Your room is narrower **than** my room. My town is quieter **than** London.

Adjectives with two syllables that end in a consonant + *-y*: *ugly, busy*
Add *-ier* (we replace *-y* with *-i*) + *than*.

> This hotel is uglier **than** that hotel. Shanghai is busier **than** Kansas City.

Adjectives with two or more syllables: *expensive, beautiful, modern*
We use *more* + adjective + *than*.

> The Burj Khalifa is **more modern than** the Empire State Building. Taipei 101 is **more expensive than** the Burj Khalifa. SM Mall of Asia is **more modern than** the Metro Centre.

2 Correct the mistakes in the sentences (1–8) below.

1 The Louvre museum is popular the British Museum.

_____

2 The SM Mall of Asia is more of modern the Istanbul Cevahir.

_____

3 The Country Club Plaza is more small the Istanbul Cevahir.

_____

4 Modern buildings is uglyer that traditional buildings.

_____

5 The SM Mall of Asia taller the Metro Centre.

_____

6 Wood is more expensive that plastic.

_____

7 This street is many narrow than the main road.

_____

8 New York is more busy than Kansas City.

_____

Joining sentences with *but*

A sentence always has a subject and a verb. Use *but* to join two sentences that have a different subject.

Sentences 1 and 2:

Taipei 101 is tall. The Burj Khalifa is taller than Taipei 101.

↓

Join sentences 1 and 2 with *but*:

Taipei 101 is tall **but** the Burj Khalifa is taller than Taipei 101.

↓

Do not repeat *than* + noun phrase after a comparison:

Taipei 101 is tall **but** the Burj Khalifa is taller ~~than Taipei 101~~.

↓

New sentence:

Taipei 101 is tall **but** the Burj Khalifa is taller.

3 Join each pair of sentences below to make one sentence with *but*.

1 The Metro Centre has more floors than the Country Club Plaza. The Country Club Plaza has more restaurants than the Metro Centre.

_____

_____

2 The Istanbul Cevahir has more cinemas than the SM Mall of Asia. The SM Mall of Asia has more shops than the Istanbul Cevahir.

_____

_____

3 The Metro Centre is more modern than the Country Club Plaza. The Country Club Plaza is bigger than the Metro Centre.

_____

_____

4 The SM Mall of Asia is bigger than the Country Club Plaza. The Country Club Plaza is older than the SM Mall of Asia.

_____

_____

ACADEMIC WRITING SKILLS

Spelling: double consonants

Vowels are the letters *a, e, i, o* and *u*. The other letters in the alphabet are *consonants*: *b, c, d, f*, etc. We sometimes repeat a consonant in some comparative adjectives and some verb forms. If we repeat a consonant, we *double* it.

We double the consonant if:

- the word has one syllable
- the last two letters of the word are a vowel + a consonant
- the last consonant is not -*y*.

comparative adjectives: big → bigger, fat → fatter, thin → thinner
the -*ing* forms of some verbs: swim → swimming, run → running,
shop → shopping

1 Read the text below and correct the <u>underlined</u> words. Correct the spelling and/or add any missing capital letters.

What are <u>mals</u>?

Malls are big buildings for <u>shoping</u>. They are near big cities. Sometimes they are inside skyscrapers. Many cities have more than one mall. Malls have <u>restorants</u> and <u>sinemas</u>. The <u>restaraunts</u> are <u>biger</u> than <u>restrants</u> in the city. Some malls also have gyms and <u>swiming</u> pools.

The <u>country club plaza</u> in <u>kansas city</u> in the <u>united states</u> was the first mall in the world. It is popular today but there are <u>biger</u> malls in <u>america</u>, <u>europe</u>, the <u>gulf</u> and <u>asia</u>.

WRITING TASK

UNL**O**CK
ONLINE

WRITE A FIRST
DRAFT

EDIT

> Write a comparison of two buildings.

1 Choose two shopping malls from Table 7.1 in the Critical Thinking section.

2 Write sentences on the topics below.

1 Write the names of your malls.
2 Write the location of your malls.
3 Compare the age of your malls.
4 Compare the size of your malls.
5 Compare the number of floors in your malls.
6 Compare the number of shops in your malls.
7 Compare the number of restaurants in your malls.
8 Compare the number of cinemas in your malls.

3 Use the task checklist to review your sentences.

TASK CHECKLIST	✔
Did you compare two malls?	
Do your sentences have *than* after a comparative adjective?	
Do your comparative adjectives with one or two syllables end -*(e)r*?	
Do your comparative adjectives with one syllable that end in a vowel + a consonant have double consonants?	
Do your comparative adjectives with two syllables have *more* + adjective + *than*?	
Do your sentences which compare quantities have a subject and verb + *more* + a noun or a noun phrase + *than*?	

4 Make any necessary changes to your sentences.

OBJECTIVES REVIEW

5 Check your objectives.

I can ...

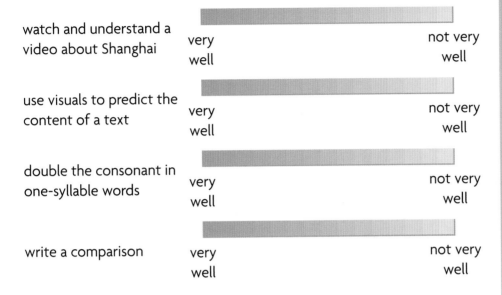

watch and understand a
video about Shanghai

very
well

not very
well

use visuals to predict the
content of a text

very
well

not very
well

double the consonant in
one-syllable words

very
well

not very
well

write a comparison

very
well

not very
well

WORDLIST

UNIT VOCABULARY	
apartment (n)	park (n)
ceiling (n)	plastic (n)
floor (= level of a building) (n)	restaurant (n)
garden (n)	roof (n)
glass (n)	room (n)
leisure centre (n)	shop (n)
lift (n)	shopping mall (n)
light (n)	swimming pool (n)
mirror (n)	tall (adj)
modern (adj)	traffic (n)
office (n)	wall (n)
open (v)	window (n)

LEARNING OBJECTIVES

Watch and listen	Watch and understand a video about food in Mexico
Reading skills	Skim
Academic writing skills	Spell adjectives for food and drink
Writing task	Write descriptive sentences

UNLOCK YOUR KNOWLEDGE

Work with a partner. Ask and answer the questions (1–3) below.

1 What is your favourite food?
2 What food is popular in your country?
3 What food is traditional in your country?

WATCH AND LISTEN

PREPARING TO WATCH

UNDERSTANDING
KEY VOCABULARY

1 Match the nouns to the definitions. Use the photos and the glossary on page 199 to help you.

1	chef	**a**	a sweet, brown food
2	market	**b**	a place where you can buy and eat food
3	restaurant	**c**	a place where people buy or sell things
4	chocolate	**d**	someone whose job is to cook food

2 Read the sentences (1–4) below and write the nouns from Exercise 1 in the gaps.

1 My dad is a _____ . He makes delicious pizzas.

2 I like eating _____ .

3 There is a new _____ in my town. You can eat Mexican food there.

4 I go to the _____ every day to buy fruit and vegetables.

WHILE WATCHING

UNDERSTANDING
MAIN IDEAS

3 ▶ You are going to watch a video about Mexican food. Watch the whole video, read the statements (1–6) below and write true (T) or false (F).

1 Chocolate comes from Mexico. _____

2 Martha Ortiz is a chef. _____

3 Martha is opening a new shop. _____

4 Victor Zapatero is a chef. _____

5 *Mole* is a sauce from Argentina. _____

6 Martha puts chocolate in the *mole* sauce. _____

UNL**O**CK READING AND WRITING SKILLS 1

4 ▶ Watch the video again. Answer the questions.

1 Where is Mexico?

_____

2 What is Mexico famous for?

_____

3 What is the biggest city in Mexico?

_____

4 What is very important to the people of Mexico?

_____

5 ▶ Watch the whole video again. Choose the correct answers (a, b or c).

1 Martha Ortiz lives in _____ .
   a Mexico City   b Guadalajara   c Monterrey

2 Martha is going to _____ .
   a a clothes shop   b the supermarket   c a market

3 Martha _____ what she wants.
   a doesn't find   b finds   c can't find

DISCUSSION

6 Work with a partner. Ask and answer the questions below.

1 What food do you usually eat with your family?
2 Can you cook? What food do you enjoy cooking?
3 What different restaurants are there in your town? Do you go to any of them? Which is your favourite?

READING 1

PREPARING TO READ

PREVIEWING

1 Look at the texts and the photographs on the opposite page. Circle the correct options.

1 The three texts are from t*he same book / different books.*
2 The photographs are of the *same / different* countries.
3 The texts come from an *international / Asian* history of tea.

UNDERSTANDING
KEY VOCABULARY

2 Write the words from the box in the gaps. Use a dictionary to help you.

> leaves   prepare   guests   tastes   pull   pour   kettle

1 Chocolate _____ very good.
2 In London, the _____ fall from the trees in autumn.
3 Can I _____ some orange juice?
4 Many Japanese chefs can _____ sushi.
5 You have to _____ the door to open it, not push!
6 I make hot water in an electric _____ .
7 There are five _____ for my birthday dinner this evening.

WHILE READING

> ### Skimming
>
> If you look for the main topic and idea of a text, you are *skimming*. When you skim, do not read every word. Read the nouns, verbs, adjectives and question words.

SKIMMING

UNLOCK ONLINE

3 Read the blue words in the texts. Write true (T) or false (F) next to the statements below.

1 The texts compare tea and coffee.   _____
2 Tea is popular in many countries.   _____
3 There is one kind of tea.   _____
4 Every country prepares and drinks tea in a different way.   _____

SCANNING TO
FIND INFORMATION

4 Scan the text. Write the names of the correct countries from the texts in the gaps.

1 People in _____ drink *teh tarik.*
2 In _____ , people prepare tea in a *samovar.*
3 People prepare tea for many hours in _____ .
4 Some people in _____ drink tea with sugar or jam.
5 People prepare tea with two kettles in _____ .
6 Tourists like watching tea sellers prepare tea in _____ .

Tea: A World History

by A. Capper

INTRODUCTION: THE WORLD IN A TEACUP

Tea is tasty and good for you. It is also one of the most popular drinks around the world. But what is tea? And why is it so popular?

All tea comes from tea leaves but tea is not always the same. There are many kinds of tea. You can drink black tea, green tea, white tea or fruit tea. Each type of tea has a different taste and a different colour.

1.1 A tea seller prepares tea in Kuala Lumpur

The history of tea begins in Asia. In China, Korea and Japan, tea is still very important today. In Japan, it can take many hours to prepare and drink tea with your guests. In Malaysia, a popular drink at breakfast is *teh tarik* ('pulled tea'). Malaysians say it is good for you and tastes good with *canai* bread.

Tourists in Kuala Lumpur like watching the tea sellers make 'pulled tea'. The tea sellers pour hot water on black tea. After five minutes, they add sugar and milk. Then they 'pull' the tea – they pour the tea from one cup to another many times.

1.4 A Russian samovar

In many countries, you must have a special kettle to make tea. People in different countries also like to add different things to their tea. For example, Russians use a special kettle called a *samovar*. They like drinking tea with lemon. Sometimes, they also drink tea with some sugar or jam.

In Turkey, tea comes in a *Çaydanlık*. A *Çaydanlık* has two kettles: one for the water and one for the tea. Drink Turkish tea with some sugar.

Arab tea, called *karak*, has cardamon, ginger, milk and sugar. In the United Kingdom, they add some milk and sugar.

The British usually eat biscuits with their tea. In Japan, they like…

1.5 A Turkish Çaydanlık set

DISCUSSION

5 Work with a partner. Ask and answer the questions (1–3) below.

1 Do you prefer tea or coffee?
2 How do people drink tea in your country? (e.g. with sugar? with milk?)
3 Do you have a favourite cold drink? (e.g. Cola)

READING 2

PREPARING TO READ

PREVIEWING

1 Look at the text and the photographs on the opposite page. Circle the correct option.

1 The text is from a website for *tourists / students*.
2 The text is about different *kinds of food / things to do* in Melbourne.

UNDERSTANDING
KEY VOCABULARY

2 Match the words in the box to the correct photographs (1–4). Use the glossary on page 199 to help you.

rice   pineapple   mushroom   cabbage

1 _____ 2 _____ 3 _____ 4 _____

3 Write the words and phrases from the box in the gaps. Use the glossary on page 199 to help you.

is served in   dish   is served with   cuisine   serves

1 A waiter _____ food and drink in a restaurant.
2 Tea _____ milk in the UK.
3 Tea _____ a glass in Russia.
4 Green curry is a famous _____ from Thailand.
5 Vegetables and rice are popular in Indian _____ .

WHILE READING

SCANNING TO
FIND INFORMATION

4 Scan the text. Write true (T) or false (F) next to the statements (1–7) below.

1 The different cuisines are in alphabetical order. _____
2 *Sharwarma* is a fish dish. _____
3 *Amok trey* is an Australian dish. _____
4 Kangaroo meat is popular in Australian restaurants. _____
5 Pineapple is popular in Arab cuisine. _____
6 There are different kinds of *kabsa*. _____
7 Arab food is served with mushrooms and cabbage. _____

www.melbourne/studentguide

Melbourne/Student Guide

Melbourne/Studentguide/Entertainment/Eating out/10 of the best

Home   The city   Map   Public transport   Culture   Entertainment   Help

10
OF THE BEST BY CUISINE

Arab cuisine

Australian cuisine

British cuisine

Cambodian cuisine

Chinese cuisine

French cuisine

Japanese cuisine

Korean cuisine

Mexican cuisine

Turkish cuisine

Melbourne is a big city. We have cuisine from all over the world. Try some!

Kabsa

Crocodile

Amok trey

Arab cuisine

At an Arab restaurant, you can find delicious lamb, chicken and beef dishes. Two popular dishes are *sharwarma* and *kabsa*. *Sharwarma* is a savoury meat dish. The meat is served in *pita* bread with tomato and cucumber. *Kabsa* is popular in many Middle Eastern countries but it is very popular in Saudi Arabia. *Kabsa* is a rice, meat and vegetable dish. There are many different ways to prepare *kabsa*. *Falafel* is …

Read more

Click here for Arab restaurants in Melbourne ►

Australian cuisine

If you are in Australia, you must try a crocodile or kangaroo dish! Many Australian restaurants serve crocodile curry. Crocodile meat is tasty and very good for you (it is better that you eat crocodile than a crocodile eats you!). Kangaroo meat is also good for you. Kangaroo burgers are served in white bread. Australian restaurants also serve great fish and other …

Read more

Click here for Australian restaurants in Melbourne ►

British cuisine ►

Cambodian cuisine

At a Cambodian restaurant, there is a lot of fruit. You can find mangoes, melons and pineapples. Cambodians also like fish with rice or noodles. Cambodian dishes are served with a lot of vegetables. Mushrooms and cabbage are very popular in Cambodian cuisine. One famous dish is *amok trey*. Cambodians prepare *amok trey* with fish, nuts, coconut milk and egg. Another dish is …

Read more

Click here for Cambodian restaurants in Melbourne ►

5 Read the text and answer the questions.

1 Where is *kabsa* a very popular dish?

_____

2 Which dish(es) is/are served in bread?

_____

3 Which kind(s) of meat is/are healthy?

_____

4 Which cuisine(s) has/have rice dishes?

_____

5 Which cuisine(s) has/have fish dishes?

_____

DISCUSSION

6 Work with a partner. Ask and answer the questions below.

1 What is your favourite meal: breakfast, lunch or dinner? Why?
2 What food don't you like? Why?
3 What is the national food in your country?
4 Do young and old people eat different kinds of food in your country? Why / Why not?

UNL✿CK READING AND WRITING SKILLS 1

◉ LANGUAGE DEVELOPMENT

VOCABULARY FOR FOOD AND DRINK

1 Write the words from the box under the correct photographs.
Use a dictionary to help you.

> potatoes   dates   milk   honey   onion   chillis
> spices   butter   almonds   yoghurt   water   coconut

1 _____   2 _____   3 _____   4 _____

5 _____   6 _____   7 _____   8 _____

9 _____   10 _____   11 _____   12 _____

Countable and uncountable nouns

Countable nouns can have a singular or a plural form and a singular or plural verb.

This **apple is** green. Some **apples are** red. This **dish is** popular in China. Many Chinese **dishes are** served with rice.

Uncountable nouns have a singular form and a singular verb. They do not have a plural form or verb.

Fish is good for you. ~~Fishes are good for you.~~
Rice is served with many Indian dishes. ~~Rices are served with many Indian dishes.~~

2 Read the sentences (1–12) below. Put a tick (✓) if they are correct and a cross (✗) if they are wrong.

1 Honeys are sweet.
2 Onions are popular in European cuisine.
3 Milks are good for children.
4 Chillis are spicy.
5 Dates are served with coffee in Saudi Arabia.
6 Potatoes are in many kinds of soup.
7 Spices taste good in food.
8 Butters are served with bread.
9 Yoghurts are served with many Middle Eastern dishes.
10 Coconuts have milk.
11 Almonds are popular in sweet dishes
12 Waters are served in a glass.

3 Correct the wrong sentences in Exercise 2.

CRITICAL THINKING

UNDERSTAND

At the end of this unit, you will write descriptive sentences. Look at this unit's writing task in the box below.

Write about food in your country for a student website.

Brainstorming

If you plan or create ideas in a group you are *brainstorming*. Students can work in small groups to create a list of words about a topic.

1 Look at the notes made by a group of French students. Answer the questions.

    1 What is the topic?

    2 What does C mean?

    3 What does UC mean?

steak frites	crème brûlée
beef UC	sugar UC
chips C	eggs C
+ sauce – hollandaise	cream UC
hollandaise sauce UC	
eggs C	
butter UC	
lemon juice UC	
pepper UC	

2 Read the text and write the words from the notes in Exercise 1 in the gaps.

10
OF THE
BEST BY
CUISINE

Arab cuisine
Australian cuisine
British cuisine
Cambodian cuisine
Chinese cuisine
French cuisine
Japanese cuisine
Korean cuisine
Mexican cuisine
Turkish cuisine

Melbourne is a big city.
We have cuisine from all over
the world. Try some!

At a French restaurant, you can find many different kinds of soup and sauce. Meat and fish dishes are very popular. French cuisine is also famous for its different kinds of bread and cheese. Two popular dishes are (1) _____ and (2)_____ . *Steak frites* is a delicious meat dish. It is beef served with (3) _____ . It is also served with hollandaise sauce. French chefs prepare hollandaise sauce with eggs, (4) _____ , lemon juice and (5) _____ . *Crème brûlée* is a sweet dish. Chefs prepare it with eggs, (6) _____ and sugar …

Read more

3 Work in small groups. Brainstorm the food in two popular dishes from your country.

4 Look at your notes. Write C next to countable nouns and UC next to uncountable nouns. Use a dictionary to help you.

WRITING

GRAMMAR FOR WRITING

Subject–Verb agreement

A sentence must have a subject and a verb. The *subject* can be singular or plural. The verb must *agree* with the subject.

Use a singular verb form with a singular subject and a plural verb form with a plural subject.

singular: This child is happy. It is a popular dish. Vietnamese cuisine uses coconut milk.

plural: The children are happy. They are popular dishes. Asian cuisines use coconut milk.

Remember: uncountable nouns must have a singular verb form (see Language Development, page 150).

UNLOCK
ONLINE

1 Circle the correct verb form.

1 Turkish chefs *prepare / prepares* small dishes called *meze*.
2 Emirati cuisine *use / uses* a lot of fish.
3 A famous dish in Japan *is / are* sushi.
4 Fish *is / are* popular in many restaurants in Istanbul.
5 Chinese food *is / are* served with rice and vegetables.
6 Two popular rice dishes in Thailand *is / are* called 'khao mok kai' and 'khao na pet'.

2 Read the sentences (1–6) below. Put a tick (✓) if they are correct and a cross (✗) if they are wrong. Use a dictionary to help you.

1 Egyptian restaurants serves falafel with cucumber sauce.
2 Hummus is served with bread.
3 Nigerian chefs prepares pepper soup with fish or meat.
4 Hamburgers is served in bread.
5 Pineapples and mangoes are sweet.
6 French onion soup are delicious.

3 Correct the wrong sentences in Exercise 2.

EXPLANATION

Determiners: *a*, *an* and *some*

Articles are *a*, *an*, *the* and 'the zero article'. Write articles before a noun or noun phrase.

Use the articles *a /an* before a singular countable noun. Do not use *a /an* before an uncountable noun. Use *a* before a consonant sound. Use *an* before a vowel sound.

> A famous dish from Italy is risotto. Amok trey is a popular Cambodian dish.
> Jumbalaya is an American dish. An apple is served with this dish.
> ~~Add a honey to the dish. English people drink tea with a milk.~~
> Add honey to the dish. English people drink tea with milk.

You can use *some* before:

- a plural countable noun
- an uncountable noun.

Some means 'more than one' before a countable noun. *Some* means 'a (small) part of' before an uncountable noun.

> Some dates are served with the coffee. Chefs prepare the dish with some lemons.
> Add some honey to the dish. English people drink tea with some milk.

4 Correct the <u>underlined</u> parts of the sentences (1–8) below.

1 At <u>some Arab restaurant,</u> you can find delicious beef dishes.

_____

2 The curry is served with <u>a rice</u>.

_____

3 <u>Some famous dish</u> in New Orleans <u>is</u> *jambalaya* and *gumbo*.

_____

4 French chefs add <u>a apple</u> to this dish.

_____

5 Emirati chefs prepare *harees* with <u>a meat</u> or <u>a chicken</u>.

_____

6 <u>Australian</u> like eating <u>a crocodile meat</u>.

_____

7 There are <u>some carrot</u> in Korean *kim chee*.

_____

8 <u>Some popular dish</u> in Lagos is pepper soup.

_____

ACADEMIC WRITING SKILLS

SPELLING

1 Look at the words below. Write *a*, *e*, *i*, *o* or *u* to spell adjectives for food and drink.

1 I love sw __ __ t foods like dates.
2 I prefer to eat s __ v __ ry foods with more salt than sugar.
3 My mother's cakes are always d __ l __ c __ __ __ s!
4 I don't like green chillis. They are too sp __ cy.
5 I try to eat h __ __ lthy foods like vegetables and fruit.
6 *Kabsa* is so t __ sty. I always want more.

2 Choose the correct spelling.

1 My favourite food is _____ .
   a chocolate   **b** shocolat   **c** chokilat
2 Most people in my country buy food from the _____ .
   a markit   **b** market   **c** markat
3 I know how to _____ my national food.
   a prepear   **b** prepare   **c** brebar
4 We make a special _____ using milk.
   a sause   **b** sowse   **c** sauce
5 My grandfather grows _____ in his garden.
   a abbels   **b** appols   **c** apples
6 Most people where I live eat _____ on Fridays.
   a meat   **b** meet   **c** meed

WRITING TASK

> Write about food in your country for a student website.

1 Look at the brainstorming notes you made for Exercise 3 in the Critical Thinking section.

2 Write answers that are true for your dishes in the gaps.

_____ (*which?*) cuisine
At a _____ (*which?*) restaurant,
you find many different kinds of _____
_____ (*what kinds of food?*).
_____ (*what kind of dishes?*) are
very popular. _____ (*which?*) food is
also famous for _____ (*what kind of
food or what kind of dishes?*).

_____

_____

_____

_____

_____

_____

_____

_____

_____

_____

_____

_____

3 Write sentences about two popular dishes in your country. Add them to your text above.

4 Use the task checklist to review your sentences.

TASK CHECKLIST	✔
Do your sentences describe two popular dishes in your country?	
Do subjects and verbs agree in your sentences?	
Do the uncountable nouns have a singular form?	
Do the uncountable nouns have a singular verb?	
Is the article *a/an* before a singular countable noun?	
Is *some* before a plural countable noun or an uncountable noun?	

5 Make any necessary changes to your sentences.

OBJECTIVES REVIEW

6 Check your objectives.

I can ...

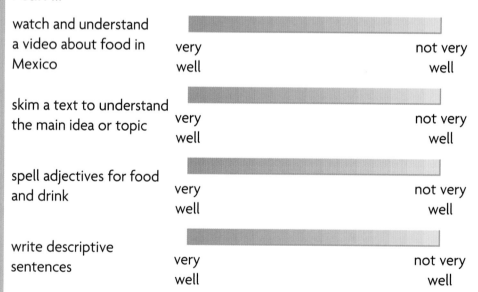

watch and understand
a video about food in
Mexico

very
well

not very
well

skim a text to understand
the main idea or topic

very
well

not very
well

spell adjectives for food
and drink

very
well

not very
well

write descriptive
sentences

very
well

not very
well

WORDLIST

UNIT VOCABULARY	
apple (n)	market (n)
banana (n)	meat (n)
bread (n)	mushroom (n)
carrot (n)	orange (n)
chef (n)	pepper (n)
chocolate (n)	potato (n)
dish (n)	prepare (v)
egg (n)	rice (n)
fish (n)	sauce (n)
mango (n)	serve (v)

LEARNING OBJECTIVES

Watch and listen	Watch and understand a video about wildlife in South Africa
Reading skills	Read for the main ideas
Academic writing skills	Use correct spelling and punctuation in sentences
Writing task	Write a descriptive paragraph

UNL⊘CK YOUR KNOWLEDGE

Write the words from the box in the gaps. Use a dictionary to help you understand the words in **bold**.

bee   bear   penguin   snake

1 A _____ is a **reptile**.
2 A _____ is an **insect**.
3 A _____ is a **mammal**.
4 A _____ is a **bird**.

WATCH AND LISTEN

PREPARING TO WATCH

USING YOUR
KNOWLEDGE TO
PREDICT CONTENT

1 Work in small groups. You are going to watch a video about wildlife in South Africa. Before you watch, write the names of three animals you think you will see.

1 _____

2 _____

3 _____

2 Watch the video with no sound. What animals can you see?

UNDERSTANDING
KEY VOCABULARY

3 Check the meanings of the words in the box. Use a dictionary to help you.

> diversity   savannah   species   grass   powerful   unusual

4 Read the definitions (1–6) below and write the words from the box in the gaps.

1 _____ : a group of plants or animals that are all similar

2 _____ : very strong

3 _____ : different from typical things

4 _____ : when many different kinds of people or things are in one place

5 _____ : a plant with small green or yellow leaves found in gardens and fields

6 _____ : land in Africa with no people or cities

WHILE WATCHING

LISTENING FOR KEY INFORMATION

5 ▶ Watch the video with sound and make notes. Write the adjectives you hear for each animal in column A.

animals	A adjectives	B numbers
springboks		
lions and elephants		
rhinos		
penguins		

6 ▶ Watch again. Write the numbers you hear for rhinos and penguins in column B.

7 Match the numbers in your notes to the information below. There are many numbers in the video. Make sure you have the correct number for each answer.

a _____ = the number of animals on a beach in Cape Town

b _____ = the speed of an animal in kilometres per hour (kph)

c _____ = an animal's weight in kilograms (kg)

DISCUSSION

8 Work with a partner. Ask and answer the questions (1–3) below.

1 Do you have a favourite animal?
2 What animal(s) are popular in your country?
3 Do you have a pet at home (e.g. a cat, some fish)?

PREPARING TO READ

PREVIEWING

1 Look at the text and the photographs on the opposite page. Circle the correct words.

1 The text is for *school children / university students*.
2 The text is about *typical / unusual* kinds of animals.

UNDERSTANDING KEY VOCABULARY

2 Read the sentences (1–7) and write the words from the box in the gaps. Use the glossary on page 200 to help you.

> lays eggs   strange   romantic   weighs   variety   Kingdom   long

1 Ayşe and her mother like watching _____ movies.
2 England and Wales are two of the countries in the United _____ .
3 I have a chicken. It _____ every morning.
4 The average healthy man _____ about 70 kg.
5 'Your cat is pink! That is very _____ !'
6 An average car in the US is four metres _____ .
7 Hamdan likes a _____ of different cuisines – Emirati, French and Korean.

WHILE READING

READING FOR MAIN IDEAS

3 Read only the highlighted topic sentences in the text. Circle the correct answer (a–c).
The main topic of the text is

a animals in Australia
b birds in New Zealand
c unusual animals around the world

UNLOCK ONLINE

Reading for the main ideas

Many texts have *paragraphs*. A paragraph is part of a long text. A paragraph has two or more sentences. Each paragraph has a *topic sentence*.

The topic sentence is usually the first sentence in a paragraph. It is important because it has the main idea for the paragraph. The highlighted sentences in Reading 1 are the topic sentences.

4 Read the text and answer the questions (1–4) below.

1 Why is the kakapo parrot unusual?
2 Why is the kiwi 'romantic'?
3 Why is the platypus an unusual mammal?
4 How big is the bumblebee bat?

Variety in the Animal Kingdom

Erik J. Cunliffe

NATIONAL UNIVERSITY OF NEW ZEALAND PRESS
AUCKLAND • LONDON • NEW YORK

Introduction

There are about 10 million different kinds of animal on earth and they come in all shapes and sizes. This book is a simple introduction to the huge variety in the animal kingdom. It features some of the most unusual animals in the world and includes key data on each species and their habits in the wild.

Some of the strangest animals in the world live in Australia and New Zealand. There is the kakapo parrot (*Strigops habroptila*). It is a bird but it cannot fly. It is a nocturnal animal. It sleeps in the day and eats at night. There are only 131 kakapo parrots in the world.

Kakapo parrot

The kiwi (*Apteryx australis*) is another bird that cannot fly. Some birds are very beautiful – but the kiwi is not. It is one of the ugliest birds in the world. But the kiwi is the most romantic bird in the world. Male and female kiwis live together for 30 years.

Kiwi

Australia has many strange animals. The most surprising Australian animal is the platypus (*Ornithorhynchus anatinus*). It has the face and feet of a bird, the body of a rat and the tail of a beaver. It is a mammal but it lays eggs.

Platypus

The smallest mammal in the world lives in Asia. It is the bumblebee bat (*Craseonycteris thonglongyai*). It lives in Thailand. It is only 2.5 cm long and it weighs 3 g. There are only 2,000 bumblebee bats left in Thailand because people burn the forest where they live.

Bumblebee bat

PREPARING TO READ

1 Match the sentence halves. Use the glossary on page 200 to help you understand the words in bold.

1 The average healthy person can	a fish in rivers.
2 Young **wolves**, lions and	b **prey** in jungles.
3 Bears can swim and they **catch**	c ten long arms.
4 Lions **hunt**	d **run** at about 10 kph.
5 Birds, bats and some insects	e dangerous **hunters** in the world.
6 Tigers look for their	f zebras.
7 **Squid** live in the sea and have	g have **wings**.
8 People are the most	h bears are called **cubs**.

2 Look at the title of a magazine article. Which animals do you think are the world's fastest hunters?

The World's Fastest Hunters

WHILE READING

3 Skim the texts. Which three animals are the fastest hunters?

4 Scan the three texts. Write the information from the texts in the table below.

scientific name	*Acinonyx jubatus*	*Istiophorus albicans* and *Istiophorus platypterus*	*Falco peregrinus*
common name			
size (cm)			
weight (kg)			
lifespan (years)			
speed (kph)			
habitat			
prey			

5 There are six paragraphs in the three texts. In one paragraph, the topic sentence is the second sentence. Which paragraph?

A

Cheetahs (*Acinonyx jubatus*) are the fastest animals on land. They can run at 112 kph. They are smaller than lions and leopards. The average cheetah is 66 cm to 99 cm high and weighs between 35 and 72 kg. Cheetahs live for about 12 years. Female cheetahs usually look after their cubs alone. They usually have between two and four cubs.

Cheetahs use their speed to catch their prey. They hunt gazelles and zebras. In the past, cheetahs lived in Asia, the Middle East and Africa. Now, most cheetahs live in East Africa but there are a small number of cheetahs in Iran.

B

Sharks may be the most dangerous animal in the sea, but they are not the fastest swimmers. The fastest swimmers are sailfish. There are two kinds of sailfish. Atlantic sailfish (*Istiophorus albicans*) live in the Atlantic Ocean, and Indo-Pacific sailfish (*Istiophorus platypterus*) live in the Indian Ocean and the Pacific Ocean.

Sailfish can swim at 109 kph. Sailfish hunt other fish and squid. They often hunt in groups. The biggest sailfish are 3 m long and weigh 90 kg. The average sailfish is usually smaller than this. They live for about four years.

C

Peregrine falcons (*Falco peregrinus*) are the fastest birds on earth. They usually fly at 65–90 kph but they can fly faster when they hunt. Their highest speed is about 325 kph. They hunt other birds – usually ducks and pigeons. Their wings are about 120 cm long. Their body is about 34–58 cm long. They weigh about 1 kg.

You can see peregrine falcons in most countries. They can live in very cold and very hot places. They live for about 15 years.

EXPLANATION

can and *cannot*

We use *can* + infinitive to show that an action is possible. We use *cannot* + infinitive to show that an action is not possible.

> They **can** run at 112 kph. Sailfish **can** swim at 109 kph. They **can** live in very cold and very hot places.
> There are birds that **cannot** fly. It is a bird but it **cannot** fly.

1 Read the sentences (1–6) below and correct the mistakes in the <u>underlined</u> parts.

1 A wolf <u>can talks</u> to other wolves.

_____

2 Wolves <u>can smelling</u> blood.

_____

3 The average wolf <u>cans weigh</u> 60 kg.

_____

4 Wolves <u>cannot to climb</u> trees.

_____

5 Wolves <u>can to hunt</u> very big animals.

_____

6 A wolf <u>no can live</u> in hot countries.

_____

DESCRIBING FACTS ABOUT ANIMALS

2 Read the sentences (1–8) below and write the words from the box in the gaps.

> long   weighs   at (x2)   for   on   high   in

1 Leopards can run _____ about 60 kph.
2 An average elephant _____ about 5,500 kg.
3 Bats live _____ small insects.
4 A wolf's body is usually from 90 cm to 160 cm _____ .
5 Zebras are about 120–130 cm _____ .
6 Kangaroos live _____ Australia.
7 Bears can live _____ 25 to 30 years.
8 Eagles can fly _____ more than 75 kph.

3 Match the words (a–h) below to the sentences (1–8) in Exercise 2.

a habitat   _____
b size (height)   _____
c size (length)   _____
d lifespan   _____
e speed (on land)   _____
f weight   _____
g speed (in the air) _____
h prey/diet   _____

VOCABULARY FOR ANIMALS

4 Match the sentence halves. Use a dictionary to help you understand the words in bold.

1 Some **spiders** are
2 The crocodile is one of the
3 Tigers are an
4 People do not like **snakes** but
5 Bats are **nocturnal** animals.
6 Frogs are **amphibious**.

a many of them are **harmless**.
b They can live on land and in water.
c **venomous**.
d **endangered** species.
e They hunt at night.
f **deadliest** animals in the world.

CRITICAL THINKING

At the end of this unit, you will write a descriptive paragraph. Look at this unit's writing task in the box below.

> Write a paragraph about an animal.

1 Read the data in Table 9.1. Use a dictionary to help you understand the words in bold.

Table 9.1: Three types of bear

scientific name	*Ailuropoda melanoleuca*	*Ursus maritimus*	*Ursus arctos*
common name	panda bear	polar bear	brown bear
size (cm)	120–180	250–300	150–250
weight (kg)	100–115	350–480	300–335
running speed (kph)	12–15	35–40	40–45
lifespan (years)	c. 20–30	c. 23–25	c. 22–24
diet	bamboo	seals	fish, **nuts**, fruit
habitat	China	**Arctic Circle**	USA, Canada, Europe, Asia
population	c. 1,000	c. 23,000	c. 200,000

2 Work with a partner. Ask and answer the questions (1–7) below.

1 Which type of bear is the biggest?
2 Which type of bear is the heaviest?
3 Which type of bear is the fastest?
4 Which type of bear can live the longest?
5 Which type of bear has the most varied diet?
6 Which type of bear has the biggest population?
7 Which type of bear is the most endangered?

3 Look at Table 9.1 again. Write the information from the table in the gaps below.

Polar bears (*Ursus maritimus*) may be the biggest bears, but they are not the fastest runners. The fastest running bear is the brown bear (*Ursus arctos*). The brown bear can run at about (1) _____ to 45 kph. The average brown bear is (2) _____ to (3) _____ cm high and weighs between (4) _____ and (5) _____ kg. Brown bears live for about (6) _____ to (7) _____ years. There are about (8) _____ brown bears in the world today.

Brown bears live on (9) _____ and fruit. They also hunt (10) _____ in rivers. Brown bears live in many parts of the world. They live in Europe, Asia and North America. Most brown bears live in Canada and Alaska.

WRITING

GRAMMAR FOR WRITING

Superlative adjectives

Superlative adjectives have three forms. We use *syllables* to choose the correct form. A syllable is a word or part of a word with one vowel sound.

Adjectives with one or two syllables: *small, strange*.
Write *the* + adjective + *-est* or *-st*.

> The smallest animal in the world lives in Asia. Many of the strangest animals in the world live in Australia.

Adjectives with two syllables that end consonant + *-y*: *deadly, friendly*.
Write *the* + adjective + *-iest* (replace the *-y* with *-i* and add *-est*).

> Sharks are the deadliest animal in the sea. Dolphins are the friendliest animal in the sea.

Adjectives with two or more syllables: *poisonous, endangered*.
Write *the most* + adjective.

> The most poisonous frog on earth lives in South America. The most endangered type of bear is the panda bear.

We can write the prepositional phrase *in the* + noun or *on* + noun after a superlative adjective + noun.

> The smallest animal in the world lives in Asia. Sharks are the deadliest animal in the sea. The most poisonous frog on earth lives in South America.

1 Put the words and phrases in order to make sentences.

1 fastest / in the world / horned lizard / the / is / lizard / The / .

_____

2 Sailfish / fastest / swimmers / the / are / .

_____

3 birds / on earth / are / Peregrine falcons / fastest / the / .

_____

4 kind / bear / are / Polar bears / of / biggest / the / .

_____

5 snake / sea snake / most / The / venomous / the / is / the / in / world / .

_____

6 most / butterfly / beautiful / blue Morpho butterfly / in / is / The / world / the / .

_____

7 biggest / the world / is / animal / blue whale / the / in / The / .

_____

8 wolf spider / deadliest / of / the / one / is / spiders / The / .

_____

2 Read the sentences below. Put a tick (✔) if they are correct and a cross (✗) if they are wrong.

1 Cheetahs in the world are the fastest animal.

_____

2 Cats are some of the more lazier animals in the world.

_____

3 Kakopo parrots are the more endangered kind of parrot.

_____

4 Kiwis are ugliest bird in New Zealand.

_____

5 The elephant is the biggest animal on land.

_____

6 'Mouse' spiders are some of the deadliest spiders.

_____

7 Squid in the sea are one of the strangest animals.

_____

8 The brown bear is a fastest kind of bear.

_____

3 Correct the mistakes in the sentences in Exercise 2.

ACADEMIC WRITING SKILLS

SPELLING

1 Put the letters in the correct order to make the names of animals. Use the definitions to help you.

1 tba _____ An animal like a mouse with wings which flies at night.

2 ebe _____ A yellow and black insect which makes honey.

3 nilo_____ A large animal of the cat family which lives in Africa.

4 reba_____ A large, strong animal with the Latin name Ursus.

5 rdib_____ An animal which has wings and feathers.

6 lfow_____ A wild animal of the dog family.

7 kasrh_____ A large fish with sharp teeth.

8 sicent_____ A small animal with six legs.

9 nolfca_____ A fast bird which can be trained to hunt other birds.

10 redisp_____ A small animal with eight legs which catches insects in a web.

PUNCTUATION

2 Correct the sentences (1–6) below. Add capital letters and full stops.

1 many venomous spiders live in australia

_____

2 the most venomous australian spider is also one of the smallest

_____

3 redback spiders are only 1 cm long

_____

4 the deadliest spider in australia is the redback spider

_____

5 redback spiders live on small insects

_____

6 female redback spiders live for two or three years

_____

WRITING TASK

| Write a paragraph about an animal. |

PLAN

1 Read the text about the brown bear in Exercise 3 of the Critical Thinking section again.

2 You are going to write facts about a bear. Choose the panda bear or the polar bear.

3 Write sentences on the topics below.

1 Write a sentence with the bear's common name and scientific name.

_____

_____

2 Write a sentence about the size of the bear.

_____

_____

3 Write a sentence about the weight of the bear.

_____

_____

4 Write a sentence about the speed of the bear.

_____

_____

5 Write a sentence about the lifespan of the bear.

_____

_____

6 Write a sentence about the diet of the bear.

_____

_____

7 Write a sentence about the habitat of the bear.

_____

_____

8 Write a sentence about the population of the bear.

_____

_____

4 Look at your sentences in Exercise 3 and the data in Table 9.1 in the Critical Thinking section.

1 Write two sentences with comparative adjectives.
2 Write one or two sentences with superlative adjectives.

5 Put your sentences from Exercises 3 and 4 in a paragraph. Make the topic sentence the first sentence in the paragraph.

WRITE A FIRST DRAFT

6 Use the task checklist to review your paragraph.

TASK CHECKLIST	✔
Is your paragraph about a panda bear or a polar bear?	
Is the first sentence of your paragraph a topic sentence?	
Are the facts in your sentences correct?	
Are there superlative adjectives in your paragraph?	
Are there comparative adjectives in your paragraph?	

7 Make any necessary changes to your paragraph.

OBJECTIVES REVIEW

8 Check your objectives.

I can ...

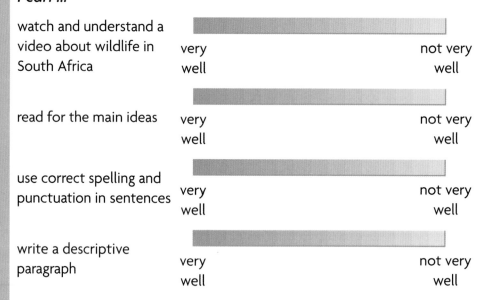

watch and understand a video about wildlife in South Africa	very well .... not very well
read for the main ideas	very well .... not very well
use correct spelling and punctuation in sentences	very well .... not very well
write a descriptive paragraph	very well .... not very well

WORDLIST

UNIT VOCABULARY		
bear (n)	lay eggs (v)	strange (adj)
bird (n)	long (adj)	unusual (adj)
catch (v)	rhino (n)	weigh (v)
cub (n)	run (v)	wing (n)
grass (n)	snake (n)	wolf (n)
hunt (v)	spider (n)	zebra (n)
insect (n)	squid (n)	

LEARNING OBJECTIVES

Watch and listen	Watch and understand a video about transport in Tokyo
Reading skills	Work out meaning from context
Academic writing skills	Understand and use error correction codes
Writing task	Write a paragraph

UNL⊙CK YOUR KNOWLEDGE

Work with a partner. Ask and answer the questions (1–4) below.

1 How do you usually travel to school or university?
2 Do you use public transport like trains or buses? Why? / Why not?
3 Which kind of transport is the safest?
4 Which kind of transport is the most dangerous?

WATCH AND LISTEN

PREPARING TO WATCH

USING VISUALS TO PREDICT CONTENT

1 You are going to watch a video about transport in Tokyo. Before you watch, look at Figures 10.1 and 10.2 below and answer the questions (1–4). Use a dictionary to help you understand the words in bold.

1 What is the most popular form of transport in Tokyo?
2 What are the two forms of **public transport?**
3 What are the two forms of **private transport?**
4 What is the distance of the **commute** between Tokyo and Sapporo?

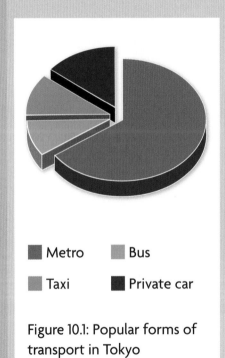

■ Metro   ■ Bus
■ Taxi   ■ Private car

Figure 10.1: Popular forms of transport in Tokyo

Figure 10.2: The Sapporo – Tokyo commute

WHILE WATCHING

2 ▶ Watch the video and take notes in the table below. Write the words for transport you see and hear the speaker say in column A.

A transport	B numbers

3 ▶ Watch again. Write the numbers you hear in column B.

4 Work with a partner. Write true (T) or false (F) next to the statements (1–5) below. Use your notes in the table to help you.

1 13 million people take taxis every day. ____
2 There are 50,000 taxis in Tokyo. ____
3 The Shinkansen bullet train travels at up to 300 kph. ____
4 Not many people commute from Sapporo to Tokyo. ____
5 10 million passengers travel to Tokyo by train every year. ____

5 Work with a partner. Read the questions (1–3) below and circle the best answers.

1 Why is the metro a popular form of transport in big cities like Tokyo, Moscow and London?
   a because it is never late
   b because there is a lot of traffic on the roads
2 Why do people fly from Sapporo to Tokyo every day?
   a because they like flying
   b because houses in Tokyo are very expensive
3 Why do people use mobile phones to check in for their flight?
   a because it is faster
   b because it is cheaper

READING 1

PREPARING TO READ

PREVIEWING

1 Work with a partner. Look at the text on the opposite page and answer the questions below.

1 What is the name of this type of text?
2 Why do people write this type of text?

USING YOUR KNOWLEDGE

2 Work with a partner. Ask and answer the questions (1–5) below.

1 Where is Bangkok?
2 Is it a big city or a small town?
3 Have you ever been to Bangkok?
4 Have you seen Bangkok in films?
5 What is the traffic like in Bangkok?

WHILE READING

SKIMMING

UNLOCK ONLINE

3 Skim the text. What information is the questionnaire trying to get? Circle the correct topics (1–6) below.

1 the number of hours people in Bangkok work or study
2 how people travel in Bangkok
3 the cost of transport in Bangkok
4 popular forms of transport in Bangkok
5 how Thai people in Bangkok travel on holiday
6 what forms of transport people own

SCANNING TO FIND INFORMATION

4 Scan the text. Write the words for transport from the text in the correct places in the table below.

land transport	water transport	air transport

READING BETWEEN THE LINES

WORKING OUT MEANING FROM CONTEXT

5 Match the highlighted words in the text to their definitions.

1 another word for *job*
2 another word for *metro*
3 another word for *questionnaire*
4 another word for *write*
5 another word for *form* or *type*
6 a word that means *man* or *woman*

Working out meaning from context

The type of text and the topic are part of the *context* of a text. You can use context to help you guess the meaning of new words.

Transport Survey

We are a group of Engineering students from Australia. This summer, we are studying at Bangkok University of Science and Technology (BUST). We would like to find out:

1   How people in Bangkok travel.
2   How people feel about transport in Bangkok.

Please answer the questions below. The survey takes about five minutes to complete.

A. About you
Tick (✔) the correct boxes to answer the questions.

A1   Age: How old are you?
   ☐ 14–17   ☐ 18–21   ☐ 22–31
   ☐ 32–53   ☐ older than 53

A2   Gender: I am ☐ Male   ☐ Female

A3   Occupation: What do you do?
   ☐ study
   ☐ work

B. Travel
Tick (✔) the correct boxes to answer the questions.

B1   How long is your journey to work or school?
   ☐ 5–15 minutes   ☐ 45–60 minutes
   ☐ 15–45 minutes   ☐ more than 1 hour

B2   How do you get to work or school?
   ☐ on foot   ☐ water taxi
   ☐ bicycle   ☐ taxi
   ☐ car   ☐ bus
   ☐ tuk-tuk   ☐ SkyTrain
   ☐ motorbike   ☐ underground

B3   How often do you use these means of transport?
   Tick (✔) the correct answers in Table 1.

Table 1

means of transport	always	often	sometimes	not often	never
on foot					
bicycle					
car					
tuk-tuk					
motorbike					
water taxi					
taxi					
bus					
SkyTrain					
underground					

B4   **Tick (✔) all the boxes that are true for you.**
   Which type or types of transport do you own?
   I own a
   ☐ bicycle   ☐ car   ☐ motorbike
   ☐ other (please write): _____

B5   What means of transport do you use when you go on holiday?
   ☐ train   ☐ plane   ☐ car   ☐ ferry

C. Opinion
C1   **Tick (✔) the correct answers.**
   Read the statements below. Do you agree or disagree with them?

Table 2

	strongly agree	agree	neither agree nor disagree	disagree	strongly disagree
There is a lot of traffic in Bangkok.					
The traffic makes me late.					
We need more public transport.					

C2   Write any comments or suggestions that you have about transport in Bangkok.

   _____

   _____

Thank you for taking the time to complete this survey.

DISCUSSION

6 Work with a partner. Ask and answer the questions below.

1 What kind of transport do people usually use in your city or town?
2 Which kinds of transport are the best and which are the worst for:
   a long journeys?   **c** places with no roads?
   b getting fit and healthy?   **d** families?

READING 2

PREPARING TO READ

PREVIEWING

1 Look at the text and the visuals on the opposite page and answer the questions (1–3) below. Circle the correct option (a–c).

1 What type of text is it?
   a a newspaper article
   b a university report
   c a letter to the writer's family
2 What is the main topic of this text?
   a culture   **b** food   **c** transport
3 Who wrote this text?
   a a student   **b** a professor   **c** a journalist

UNDERSTANDING KEY VOCABULARY

2 Read the sentences (1–7) and write the words from the box in the gaps. Use the glossary on page 200 to help you.

| pie chart | traffic jam | spend | results | prefer | percentage | full of |

1 This is the _____ sign: %.
2 A _____ is a visual that helps you compare different amounts of things.
3 I _____ coffee to tea – I think it tastes better.
4 I like cakes and biscuits but they are _____ sugar.
5 Most people _____ 30 years of their life sleeping!
6 There are so many cars! This is a very bad _____ .
7 The _____ of the English test were very good.

WHILE READING

SCANNING TO FIND INFORMATION

3 Scan the text. Write the correct numbers in the gaps on the pie chart (Figure 1).

Student Name: **Lamai Tongduan**
Student ID: **100035478 / Bangkok University of Science and Technology**
Course: **Transport and the City**

Transport in Bangkok: Report

This report shows the results of a survey of transport in Bangkok. Over 12 million people live in the city. The pie chart (Figure 1) shows the most popular means of transport in Bangkok. It shows the percentage of people who use each type of transport to get to work or school.

Every day, thousands of people use public and private transport. A popular form of transport is the SkyTrain. 21% of the population of Bangkok take the SkyTrain to work or school. Another way to travel in the city is by bus. 18% of people who live in Bangkok take buses. Most people in Bangkok drive their own cars. 14% of people ride motorbikes to get to work or take children to school. People prefer buses to tuk-tuks. Only 8% of people use tuk-tuks to get to work or school. Only 3% walk to work and only 2% cycle to work. Most offices are too far away to walk or cycle to.

The traffic in Bangkok is very heavy. The roads are full of different types of vehicle (cars, motorbikes, tuk-tuks, etc.). Most people spend more than one hour every day travelling. Almost 35% of people are late because of traffic jams. There are no traffic jams on the river. 11% of people take the river taxi.

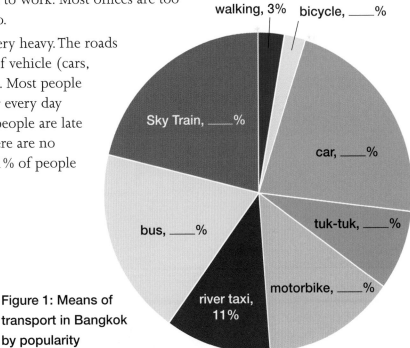

Figure 1: Means of transport in Bangkok by popularity

4 Read the text again and answer the questions (1–5) below.

1 How many people live in Bangkok?

_____

2 Is the SkyTrain a public or a private form of transport?

_____

3 Are there a lot of cars in Bangkok?

_____

4 How long is the journey to work or school for most people?

_____

5 How many people are late to work or school because of traffic jams?

_____

5 Write the words and phrases from the box in the gaps below. Use the words in bold to help you choose the answers.

> another way   vehicle   the city (x2)   who   it

This report shows the results of a survey about transport in **Bangkok**. Over 12 million people live in (1) _____ . **The pie chart** (Figure 1) shows the most popular means of transport in Bangkok. (2) _____ shows the percentage of **people** (3) _____ use each type of transport to get to work or school. Twenty-one per cent of the population of Bangkok take the SkyTrain to work or school. (4) _____ to travel in (5) _____ is by **bus**. The **traffic** in Bangkok is very heavy. The roads are full of different kinds of (6) _____ (cars, motorbikes, etc.).

◉ LANGUAGE DEVELOPMENT

EXPLANATION

Quantifiers

Quantifiers tell us the answer to the question *How many?* We use quantifiers before a noun. For small numbers, we use *a few*, *not many* and *some*. For bigger numbers, we use *many*, *a lot of* and *most*.

A few people take tuk-tuks in Bangkok.
Not many people take taxis in Tokyo.
Some trains are very fast.
Many people commute from Sapporo to Tokyo.
There are a lot of taxis in Tokyo.
Most people in Bangkok drive their own cars.

1 Read the sentences (1–5) below. Circle the quantifier and underline the noun the quantifier refers to.

1 Most people in Bangkok drive their own cars.
2 Some people ride motorbikes.
3 Not many people cycle to work or school.
4 A few people take the river taxi.
5 Many people take the SkyTrain.

2 Read the sentences (1–5) below and write quantifiers in the gaps. Use the percentages to help you. More than one answer is possible.

1 _____ (62%) people in London take the underground to work.
2 _____ (8%) people drive their cars to work in London.
3 Today, _____ (18%) people in London cycle to work.
4 _____ (9%) people in London take the bus to work.
5 _____ (3%) people in London walk or run to work.

TRANSPORT COLLOCATIONS

We can use these types of collocation when we talk about transport.

subject	verb	determiner	noun (transport)	prepositional phrase (*to* + place)
Many students My parents Commuters We	take	the their a	bus metro cars taxi	to school. to work. to the supermarket.

subject	verb	prepositional phrase (*to* + place)	prepositional phrase (*by* + noun for transport)
Many students My brothers Commuters We	travel get	to school to work to the supermarket	by bus. by metro. by car. by taxi.

3 Put the words in order to make sentences.

1 to / take / school / We / a bus / .

_____

2 travels / by / work / train / Malai / to / .

_____

3 takes / to / the city / his car / Sunan / .

_____

4 get / to / work / Many people / motorbike / by / .

_____

5 by / My children / bicycle / to / get / school / .

_____

6 a taxi / to / the mall / Suni / takes / .

_____

4 Read the sentences (1–5) and write the verbs from the box in the gaps.

ride   rides   drive   takes   flies

1 David _____ a motorbike. His mother does not like it.
2 A pilot _____ a plane.
3 Ali can _____ a camel.
4 Alison usually _____ the bus to school.
5 Saad prefers to _____ a car.

CRITICAL THINKING

At the end of this unit, you will write a paragraph. Look at this unit's writing task in the box below.

> Write a paragraph about transport in your city.

Collecting data

Before we write, we can *collect data*. *Data* are facts. We can use questionnaires and surveys to collect data.

1 Choose six forms of transport that are popular in your city. Write the words in the correct places in the questionnaire below.

UNDERSTAND

> on foot / walking camel taxi minibus bicycle taxi
> ferry metro train bus tram car
> river taxi plane motorbike

Travel

Tick (✔) the correct boxes to answer the questions.

1 How long is your journey to work or school?
   ☐ 5–15 minutes
   ☐ 16–45 minutes
   ☐ 46–60 minutes
   ☐ More than 1 hour

2 How do you get to work or school?
   ☐ _____
   ☐ _____
   ☐ _____
   ☐ _____
   ☐ _____
   ☐ _____

3 How often do you use these means of transport?
   Tick (✔) the correct answers in Table 1.

   Table 1

means of transport	always	sometimes	never
_____			
_____			
_____			
_____			
_____			
_____			

2 Make copies of your survey. Give the survey to other students in your class.

APPLY

3 Read the results of your survey. Find the percentages and then make two pie charts to show the results of Questions 1 and 2.

4 Read the results again. Write sentences that are true for your results for Question 3.

1 Most students in my class _____ .
2 Some students in my class _____ .
3 A few students in my class _____ .

WRITING

GRAMMAR FOR WRITING

Subject – Verb – Object

A sentence is about a *subject*. The subject is a *pronoun*, a *noun* or a *noun phrase*. The *verb* is after the subject in a sentence. A sentence can have an *object*. The object is a pronoun, a noun or a noun phrase. The object is after the verb.

subject: **14% of people** ride motorbikes. **11% of people** take the river taxi.
verb: 14% of people **ride** motorbikes. 11% of people **take** the river taxi.
object: 14% of people ride **motorbikes**. 11% of people take **the river taxi**.

A prepositional phrase is <u>not</u> the object of a verb.
Many students in the class travel to school by metro.
A few students in the class get to school by car.

1 Read the sentences (1–5) below. Put a tick (✔) if the bold word is an object.

1 Many commuters travel by **plane**.
2 Many commuters in Hong Kong take the **ferry** to work.
3 Students in Sharjah do not cycle to **university**.
4 In Saigon, families often ride a **motorbike** to work and school.
5 Most people in Moscow travel by **metro**.

2 Three of the sentences below have objects. Find the objects and underline them.

1 Jamila and Kamilah travel to school by car.
2 Hamdan drives a car to university.
3 Some people cycle to work in New York.
4 Many commuters ride a bicycle to work in London.
5 People in Bangkok prefer to take the SkyTrain.

UNLOCK READING AND WRITING SKILLS 1

3 Work with a partner. Correct the mistakes in the sentences (1–5) below.

1 In Abu Dhabi, commuters travel by car to work.
2 Not many people in Ankara travel to work by a taxi.
3 Commuters in Seoul take the metro work.
4 Most students to school a motorbike ride.
5 Some students in Paris drives to university.

EXPLANATION

Linking sentences with pronouns

We use *pronouns* when we do not want to repeat the same noun or noun phrase in a paragraph. The pronouns *he*, *she*, *it* and *they* can replace nouns. We can use pronouns to link *subjects* or *objects* in different sentences.

subject: **The pie chart** shows the most popular means of transport in Bangkok. ~~The pie chart~~ It shows the percentage of people who use each type of transport to get to work or school.
object: Many students ride **motorbikes**. ~~Motorbikes~~ They are not expensive.

4 Match sentences 1–5 with sentences a–e. Use the words in bold to help you.

1 **Jamila and Kamilah** travel to school by car.
2 **Hamdan** drives a car to university.
3 **Some people** cycle to work in New York.
4 Many commuters ride a **bicycle** to work in London.
5 People in Bangkok prefer to take the **SkyTrain**.

a **He** is a good driver.
b **It** is cheaper than a tuk-tuk!
c **It** is a healthy form of transport.
d **They** travel in their father's car.
e **They** can ride on special roads for bicycles.

5 Read the pairs of sentences (1–5) below and write the correct pronouns in the gaps.

1 Many commuters travel by **plane**. _____ is an expensive form of transport.
2 Many commuters in Hong Kong take the **ferry** to work. _____ is cheap and efficient.
3 **Students** in Sharjah do not cycle to university. _____ drive there.
4 In Saigon, **families** often ride a motorbike to work and school. _____ travel together.
5 Most people in Moscow travel by **metro**. _____ is the busiest underground in the world.

ACADEMIC WRITING SKILLS

Error correction

Some teachers use correction codes for errors. Look at the examples below.

[G] = grammar ~~They is from Egypt.~~ → They are from Egypt.

[MW] = missing word ~~They from Egypt.~~ → They are from Egypt.

[P] = punctuation ~~they are from egypt~~ → They are from Egypt.

[C]= content (is the information correct?) ~~They are from France.~~ → They are from Egypt.

[WP] = wrong preposition ~~They are of Egypt.~~ → They are from Egypt.

Look at a student's paragraph marked with correction codes. Correct the mistakes.

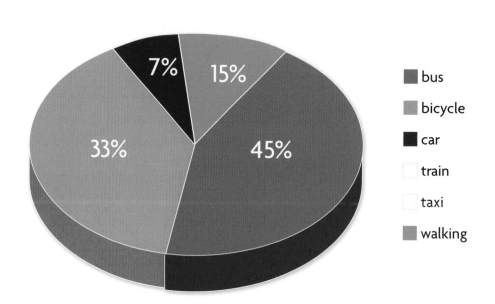

Figure 1: Popular means of transport for students in Madrid

The pie chart (Figure 1) <u>show</u> [G] popular means of transport for students ____ [MW] Madrid. There are five types of transport: bicycle, bus, car, taxi ____ [MW] train <u>most</u> [P] <u>peoples</u> [G] travel <u>in</u> [WP] bus (<u>33%</u>) [C]. Bicycles ____ [MW] also very popular. 33% of students travel to school by <u>a</u> [G] bicycle. Students prefer cars but more students own bicycles than cars. 7% of <u>student</u> [G] drive <u>for</u> [WP] school. Students do not take ____ [MW] to school. Buses are the <u>more</u> [G] popular form of transport for students in Madrid.

UNLOCK READING AND WRITING SKILLS 1

WRITING TASK

> Write a paragraph about transport in your city.

1 Look at the results of your survey and your pie charts from the Critical Thinking section.

2 You are going to use the results to write about transport in your city. Write the name of the city in the title for your paragraph and the titles of your pie charts.

  1 Transport in _____ : Report
  2 Figure 1: Average travel times in _____ .
  3 Figure 2: Popular means of transport for students in

     _____ .

3 Write your introduction. Write answers that are true for your report in the gaps below.

> This report shows the results of a survey about transport
> in _____ (*name of your city*). Over
> _____ (*population of your city*) people live
> in the city. Figure 1 shows average travel times in
> _____ (*name of your city*). Figure 2 shows the popular
> means of transport in _____ (*name of your city*).

4 Write sentences on the topics below.

  1 Write a sentence about the six forms of transport in your survey.
  2 Write three or four sentences about the percentage of people that use each form of transport.
  3 Write two or three sentences that compare popular forms of transport in the city.
  4 Write a sentence about the most popular form of transport in the city.
  5 Write one or two sentences about travel times.

5 Put your introduction and your sentences together to make a paragraph. Link your sentences with pronouns. Add your pie charts to the paragraph.

6 Use the task checklist to review your paragraph.

TASK CHECKLIST	✔
Is your paragraph is about transport in your city?	
Does your paragraph have percentages from your pie charts?	
Do pronouns link your sentences?	
Do your sentences use correct punctuation?	

7 Work with a partner. Check your partner's paragraph. Use error correction codes to mark it.

OBJECTIVES REVIEW

8 Check your objectives.

I can ...

watch and understand a video about transport in Tokyo

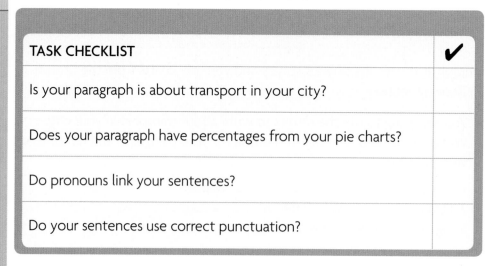

very well   not very well

work out meaning from context

very well   not very well

understand and use error correction codes

very well   not very well

write a paragraph

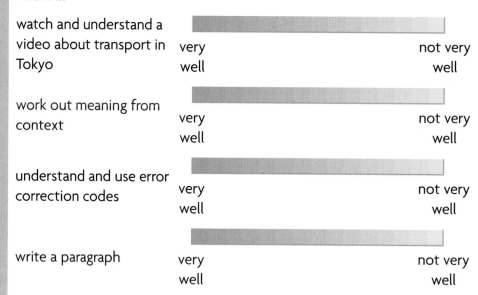

very well   not very well

WORDLIST

UNIT VOCABULARY		
complete (v)	percentage (n)	traffic (n)
full (adj)	pie chart (n)	traffic jam (n)
metro (n)	prefer (v)	the underground (n)
motorbike (n)	public transport (n)	
occupation (n)	spend (v)	

GLOSSARY

Vocabulary	Pronunciation	Part of speech	Definition
UNIT 1			
aunt	/ɑːnt/	(n)	the sister of your father or mother, or the wife of your uncle
beautiful	/ˈbjuːtɪfəl/	(adj)	very attractive
brother	/ˈbrʌðə/	(n)	a man or boy with the same parents as another person
clothes	/kləʊðz/	(n)	items such as shirts, dresses and trousers that you wear on your body
daughter	/ˈdɔːtə/	(n)	your female child
different	/ˈdɪf.ər.ənt/	(adj)	not the same
famous	/ˈfeɪ.məs/	(adj)	known or recognized by many people
farmer	/ˈfɑːmə/	(n)	someone who owns or looks after a farm
grandfather	/ˈgrændfɑːðə/	(n)	the father of a person's mother or father
grandmother	/ˈgrændmʌðə/	(n)	the mother of a person's father or mother
height	/haɪt/	(n)	how tall or high something or someone is
interesting	/ˈɪn.trəs.tɪŋ/	(adj)	someone or something that is interesting keeps your attention because they are unusual, exciting, or have lots of ideas
live	/lɪv/	(v)	to have your home somewhere
shoe	/ʃuː/	(n)	a strong covering for the foot, often made of leather
son	/sʌn/	(n)	your male child
tall	/tɔːl/	(adj)	having a greater than average height
teacher	/ˈtiːtʃə/	(n)	someone whose job is to teach in a school, college, etc.
uncle	/ˈʌŋkəl/	(n)	the brother of your mother or father, or the husband of your aunt
work	/wɜːk/	(v)	to do a job, especially the job you do to earn money
young	/jʌŋ/	(adj)	having lived or existed for only a short time and not old
UNIT 2			
autumn	/ˈɔːtəm/	(n)	the season of the year between summer and winter, when leaves fall from the trees
cloudy	/ˈklaʊdi/	(adj)	When it is cloudy, there are clouds in the sky.
cold	/kəʊld/	(adj)	having a low temperature
dangerous	/ˈdeɪndʒərəs/	(adj)	If someone or something is dangerous, they could harm you.
difficult	/ˈdɪfɪkəlt/	(adj)	when something is not easy to do or understand
dry	/draɪ/	(adj)	with no or not much rain
easy	/ˈiːzi/	(adj)	not difficult
happy	/ˈhæpi/	(adj)	feeling, showing or causing pleasure
rainy	/ˈreɪni/	(adj)	raining a lot
sad	/sæd/	(adj)	unhappy or making you feel unhappy
safe	/seɪf/	(adj)	not dangerous or likely to cause harm

Vocabulary	Pronunciation	Part of speech	Definition
spring	/sprɪŋ/	(n)	the season of the year between winter and summer, when the weather becomes warmer and plants start to grow again
summer	/'sʌmə/	(n)	the season of the year between spring and autumn, when the weather is warmest
sunny	/'sʌni/	(adj)	bright because of light from the sun
temperature	/'temprətʃə/	(n)	how hot or cold something is
warm	/wɔːm/	(adj)	having a temperature between cool and hot
windy	/'wɪndi/	(adj)	with a lot of wind
winter	/'wɪntə/	(n)	the coldest season of the year, between autumn and spring

UNIT 3

Vocabulary	Pronunciation	Part of speech	Definition
afternoon	/ɑːftə'nuːn/	(n)	the time between the middle of the day and the evening
Art	/ɑːt/	(n)	the making or study of paintings, drawings, etc. or the objects created
Biology	/baɪ'ɒlədʒi/	(n)	the scientific study of living things
Business	/'bɪznɪs/	(n)	the activity of buying and selling goods and services
café	/'kæfeɪ/	(n)	a small restaurant where you can buy drinks and light meals
car	/kɑː/	(n)	a road vehicle with an engine, four wheels, and seats for a small number of people
Chemistry	/'kemɪstri/	(n)	the scientific study of substances and the different ways in which they react or combine with other substances
cook	/kʊk/	(v)	to prepare food and usually heat it
different	/'dɪfərənt/	(adj)	not the same
early	/'ɜːli/	(adj)	before the usual time or the time that was arranged
Economics	/ikə'nɒmɪks/	(n)	the study of the way in which trade, industry and money are organized
Engineering	/endʒɪ'nɪərɪŋ/	(n)	the work of an engineer, or the study of this work
evening	/'iːvnɪŋ/	(n)	the part of the day between the afternoon and the night
Friday	/'fraɪdeɪ/	(n)	the day of the week after Thursday and before Saturday
Geography	/dʒi'ɒgrəfi/	(n)	the study of the physical surface of the Earth and all regions of the world
History	/'hɪstəri/	(n)	the study of events in the past
Humanities	/hju'mænətiz/	(n)	subjects that you study which are not connected with science, such as literature and history
late	/leɪt/	(adj)	happening or arriving after the planned, expected, usual or necessary time
Literature	/'lɪtrətʃə/	(n)	books, poems, etc. that are considered to be art
Management	/'mænɪdʒmənt/	(n)	the control and organization of something
Maths	/mæθs/	(n)	the study of numbers, shapes and space using reason and usually a special system of symbols and rules for organizing them
Monday	/'mʌndeɪ/	(n)	the day of the week after Sunday and before Tuesday

Vocabulary	Pronunciation	Part of speech	Definition
morning	/ˈmɔːnɪŋ/	(n)	the first half of the day, from the time when the sun rises or you wake up until the middle of the day
Physics	/ˈfɪzɪks/	(n)	the scientific study of matter and energy and the effect that they have on each other
Science	/ˈsaɪənts/	(n)	the study and knowledge of the structure and behaviour of natural things in an organized way
study	/ˈstʌdi/	(v)	to learn about a subject, especially on an educational course or by reading books
Tuesday	/ˈtjuːzdeɪ/	(n)	the day of the week after Monday and before Wednesday
TV	/ˈtiːviː/	(n)	television
village	/ˈvɪlɪdʒ/	(n)	a place where people live in the countryside that includes buildings such as shops but is smaller than a town
watch	/wɒtʃ/	(n)	a small clock which is worn on a strap around the wrist
Wednesday	/ˈwenzdeɪ/	(n)	the day of the week after Tuesday and before Thursday
work	/wɜːk/	(v)	to do a job, especially the job you do to earn money

UNIT 4

Vocabulary	Pronunciation	Part of speech	Definition
bank	/bæŋk/	(n)	an organization or place where you can borrow money, save money, etc.
beach	/biːtʃ/	(n)	an area of sand or small stones next to the sea
bridge	/brɪdʒ/	(n)	a structure that is built over a river, road, railway, etc. to allow people and vehicles to cross from one side to the other
capital city	/ˌkæpɪtəl ˈsɪti/	(n)	the most important city in a country or state, where the government is based
cliff	/klɪf/	(n)	a high area of rock with a very steep side, often on a coast
desert	/dezət/	(n)	a large, hot, dry area of land with very few plants
factory	/ˈfæktəri/	(n)	a building or set of buildings where large amounts of goods are made using machines
farm	/fɑːm/	(n)	an area of land with fields and buildings, used for growing crops and/or keeping animals as a business
field	/fiːld/	(n)	an area of land used for growing crops or keeping animals
fish	/fɪʃ/	(n)	an animal that lives only in water and swims using its tail and fins
forest	/ˈfɒrɪst/	(n)	a large area of trees growing closely together
fountain	/ˈfaʊntɪn/	(n)	a structure that forces water up into the air as a decoration
hill	/hɪl/	(n)	a raised area of land, smaller than a mountain
library	/ˈlaɪbrəri/	(n)	a room or building that contains a collection of books and other written material that you can read or borrow
monument	/ˈmɒnjəmənt/	(n)	an old building or place that is important in history
mountain	/ˈmaʊntɪn/	(n)	a raised part of the Earth's surface, much larger than a hill, the top of which might be covered in snow
museum	/mjuːˈziːəm/	(n)	a building where you can look at important objects connected with art, history or science

Vocabulary	Pronunciation	Part of speech	Definition
park	/pɑːk/	(n)	a large area of grass and trees in a city or town, where people can walk and enjoy themselves
river	/ˈrɪvə/	(n)	a long, natural area of water that flows across the land and into a sea, lake or another river
road	/rəʊd/	(n)	a long, hard surface built for vehicles to drive on
school	/skuːl/	(n)	a place where children go to be educated
sea	/siː/	(n)	a large area of salt water
shop	/ʃɒp/	(n)	a building or part of a building where you can buy things
train station	/ˈtreɪn ˌsteɪʃən/	(n)	a building where trains stop so that you can get on or off them
university	/juːnɪˈvɜːsiti/	(n)	a place where students study at a high level to get a degree
valley	/ˈvæli/	(n)	an area of low land between hills or mountains, often with a river running through it

UNIT 5

Vocabulary	Pronunciation	Part of speech	Definition
baseball	/ˈbeɪsbɔːl/	(n)	a game in which two teams try to win points by hitting a ball and running around four fixed points
basketball	/ˈbɑːskɪtbɔːl/	(n)	a game in which two teams try to score points by throwing a ball through a high net, or the ball used in this game
boring	/ˈbɔːrɪŋ/	(adj)	not interesting or exciting
cheap	/tʃiːp/	(adj)	costing little money or less than is usual or expected
competition	/kɒmpəˈtɪʃən/	(n)	an organized event in which people try to win a prize by being the best, fastest, etc.
exciting	/ɪkˈsaɪtɪŋ/	(adj)	making you feel very happy and enthusiastic
exercise	/ˈeksəsaɪz/	(n)	physical activity that you do to make your body strong and healthy
expensive	/ɪkˈspensɪv/	(adj)	costing a lot of money
famous	/ˈfeɪməs/	(adj)	known and recognized by many people
fan	/fæn/	(n)	someone who admires and supports a person, sport, sports team, etc.
horse riding	/ˈhɔːs ˌraɪdɪŋ/	(n)	the sport or activity of riding a horse
ice skating	/ˈaɪskeɪtɪŋ/	(n)	the activity or sport of moving across ice using ice skates
jogging	/dʒɒgɪŋ/	(n)	when you jog
judo	/dʒuːdəʊ/	(n)	a sport from Japan in which two people try to throw each other to the ground
karate	/kərɑːti/	(n)	a sport from Japan in which people fight with the hands or feet
martial art	/ˈmɑːʃəlɑːt/	(n)	a sport that is a traditional Japanese or Chinese form of fighting or defending yourself
national	/ˈnæʃənəl/	(adj)	relating to or typical of a whole country and its people
online	/ˈɒnlaɪn/	(adj)	describes products, services or information that can be bought or used on the Internet
player	/ˈpleɪə/	(n)	someone who takes part in a game or sport
squash	/skwɒʃ/	(n)	a sport in which two people hit a small rubber ball against the four walls of a room
team game	/ˈtiːm ˌgeɪm/	(n)	a sport played by a group of people against another group of players

Vocabulary	Pronunciation	Part of speech	Definition
tennis	/ˈtenɪs/	(n)	a sport in which two or four people hit a small ball to each other over a net
ticket	/ˈtɪkɪt/	(n)	a small piece of paper that shows you have paid to do something; for example, travel on a bus, watch a film, etc.

UNIT 6

Vocabulary	Pronunciation	Part of speech	Definition
bicycle	/ˈbaɪsɪkəl/	(n)	a two-wheeled vehicle that you sit on and move by turning the two pedals
building	/ˈbɪldɪŋ/	(n)	a structure with walls and a roof such as a house or factory, or the business of making these
cook	/kʊk/	(n)	someone who prepares and cooks food
friendly	/ˈfrendli/	(adj)	behaving in a pleasant, kind way towards someone
great	/greɪt/	(adj)	very good
healthy	/ˈhelθi/	(adj)	good for your health
hospital	/ˈhɒspɪtəl/	(n)	a place where ill or injured people go to be treated by doctors and nurses
kitchen	/ˈkɪtʃɪn/	(n)	a room where food is kept, prepared and cooked and where the dishes are washed
lunch	/lʌntʃ/	(n)	a meal that is eaten in the middle of the day
manager	/ˈmænɪdʒə/	(n)	someone in control of an office, shop, team, etc.
medicine	/ˈmedsən/	(n)	treatment for illness or injury, or the study of this
nurse	/nɜːs/	(n)	someone whose job is to care for ill and injured people
paint	/peɪnt/	(v)	to cover a surface with paint
software	/ˈsɒftweə/	(n)	programs that you use to make a computer do different things
soon	/suːn/	(adv)	after a short period of time

UNIT 7

Vocabulary	Pronunciation	Part of speech	Definition
apartment	/əˈpɑːtmənt/	(n)	a set of rooms for living in, especially on one floor of a building
ceiling	/ˈsiːlɪŋ/	(n)	the surface of a room which you can see when you look above you
floor	/flɔː/	(n)	a particular level of a building
garden	/ˈgɑːdən/	(n)	a piece of land belonging to a house, where flowers and other plants are grown
glass	/glɑːs/	(n)	a hard transparent substance that objects such as windows and bottles are made of
leisure centre	/ˈleʒə ˌsentə/	(n)	a building with a swimming pool and places where you can play sports
lift	/lɪft/	(n)	a machine that carries people up and down in tall buildings
light	/laɪt/	(n)	a piece of equipment which produces light, such as a lamp or a light bulb
mirror	/ˈmɪrə/	(n)	a piece of glass with a shiny metallic material on one side which produces an image of anything that is in front of it
modern	/ˈmɒdən/	(adj)	using the newest ideas, design, technology, etc. and not traditional
office	/ˈɒfɪs/	(n)	a room or building where people work

Vocabulary	Pronunciation	Part of speech	Definition
open	/ˈəʊpən/	(v)	If a shop or office opens at a particular time of day, it starts to do business at that time.
park	/pɑːk/	(n)	a large area of grass and trees in a city or town, where people can walk and enjoy themselves
plastic	/ˈplæstɪk/	(n)	a light, artificial substance that can be made into different shapes when it is soft
restaurant	/ˈrestərɔ̃ŋ/	(n)	a place where you can buy and eat a meal
roof	/ruːf/	(n)	the surface that covers the top of a building or vehicle
room	/ruːm/	(n)	a part of the inside of a building that is separated from other parts by walls, floor and ceiling
shop	/ʃɒp/	(n)	a building or part of a building where you can buy things
shopping mall	/ˈʃɒpɪŋ ˌmæl/	(n)	a large, covered shopping area
swimming pool	/ˈswɪmɪŋ ˌpuːl/	(n)	an area of water that has been made for people to swim in
tall	/tɔːl/	(adj)	having a greater than average height
traffic	/ˈtræfɪk/	(n)	the cars, trucks, etc. using a road
wall	/wɔːl/	(n)	a vertical structure, often made of stone or brick, that divides or surrounds something
window	/ˈwɪndəʊ/	(n)	a space usually filled with glass in the wall of a building or in a vehicle, to allow light and air in and to allow people inside the building to see out

UNIT 8

apple	/ˈæpəl/	(n)	a hard, round fruit that has a green or red skin and is white inside
banana	/bəˈnɑːnə/	(n)	a long curved fruit with a yellow skin
bread	/bred/	(n)	a basic food made by mixing flour, water and sometimes yeast
carrot	/ˈkærət/	(n)	a long, thin orange vegetable that grows in the ground
cheese	/tʃiːz/	(n)	a food made from milk, which can either be firm or soft and is usually yellow or white in colour
chef	/ʃef/	(n)	a skilled and trained cook who works in a hotel or restaurant, especially the most important cook
chocolate	/ˈtʃɒklət/	(n)	a sweet, brown food that is usually sold in a block
dish	/dɪʃ/	(n)	food prepared in a particular way as part of a meal
egg	/eg/	(n)	an oval object with a hard shell which is produced by female birds, especially chickens, and which is eaten as food
fish	/fɪʃ/	(n)	an animal that lives only in water and swims using its tail and fins
mango	/ˈmæŋgəʊ/	(n)	a tropical fruit that has a green skin and is orange inside
meat	/miːt/	(n)	muscles and other soft parts of animals, used as food
mushroom	/ˈmʌʃruːm/	(n)	a type of fungus with a short stem and a round top, some types of which can be eaten
orange	/ˈɒrɪndʒ/	(n)	a round, sweet fruit with a thick skin and a centre that is divided into many equal parts

Vocabulary	Pronunciation	Part of speech	Definition
pepper	/ˈpepə/	(n)	a black, grey, white or red powder produced by crushing dry peppercorns, which is used to give food a spicy flavour
potato	/pətˈeɪtəʊ/	(n)	a round vegetable with a brown, yellow, or red skin that grows in the ground
prepare	/prɪˈpeə/	(v)	to make food ready to be eaten
rice	/raɪs/	(n)	small grains from a plant that are cooked and eaten
sauce	/sɑːs/	(n)	a thick liquid eaten with food to add flavour
serve	/sɜːv/	(v)	to give someone food or drink, especially guests or customers in a restaurant or bar

UNIT 9

Vocabulary	Pronunciation	Part of speech	Definition
bear	/beə/	(n)	a large, strong, wild animal with thick fur
bird	/bɜːd/	(n)	an animal that has wings and feathers, and is usually able to fly
catch	/kætʃ/	(v)	to take hold of something, especially something that is moving through the air
cub	/kʌb/	(n)	a young bear, fox, lion, etc.
grass	/grɑːs/	(n)	a common plant with narrow green leaves that grows close to the ground
hunt	/hʌnt/	(v)	to chase and kill wild animals
insect	/ˈɪnsekt/	(n)	a small creature with six legs; for example, a bee or a fly
lay eggs	/ˌleɪ ˈegz/	(v)	If an animal lays eggs, it produces them out of its body.
long	/lɒŋ/	(adj)	used when asking for or giving information about the distance of something
rhino	/ˈraɪnəʊ/	(n)	rhinoceros
run	/rʌn/	(v)	to move on your feet at a faster speed than walking
snake	/sneɪk/	(n)	a long, thin creature with no legs that slides along the ground
spider	/ˈspaɪdə/	(n)	a small creature with eight long legs which catches insects in a web (= structure like a net)
squid	/skwɪd/	(n)	a sea creature with a long body and ten long arms
strange	/streɪndʒ/	(adj)	If something is strange, it is surprising because it is unusual or unexpected.
unusual	/ʌnˈjuʒəl/	(adj)	different and not ordinary, often in a way that is interesting or exciting
weigh	/weɪ/	(v)	to have a heaviness of a stated amount, or to measure the heaviness of an object
wing	/wɪŋ/	(n)	the flat part of the body that a bird uses for flying
wolf	/wʊlf/	(n)	a wild animal like a large dog
zebra	/zebrə/	(n)	an African animal like a horse with black and white lines

UNIT 10

Vocabulary	Pronunciation	Part of speech	Definition
complete	/kəmˈpliːt/	(v)	to write all the details asked for on a form or other document
full	/fʊl/	(adj)	containing a lot of things or people or a lot of something

Vocabulary	Pronunciation	Part of speech	Definition
metro	/ˈmetrəʊ/	(n)	an underground railway system in a large city
motorbike	/ˈməʊtəbaɪk/	(n)	a vehicle with two wheels and an engine
occupation	/ˌɒkjəˈpeɪʃən/	(n)	someone's job
percentage	/pəˈsentɪdʒ/	(n)	an amount of something, often expressed as a number out of 100
pie chart	/ˈpaɪ ˌtʃɑːt/	(n)	a circle which is divided from its centre into several parts to show how a total amount is divided up
prefer	/prɪˈfɜː/	(v)	to like someone or something more than another person or thing
public transport	/ˌpʌblɪk ˈtrænspɔːt/	(n)	a system of vehicles such as buses and trains which operate at regular times on fixed routes and are used by the public
spend	/spend/	(v)	to use time doing something or being somewhere
traffic	/ˈtræfɪk/	(n)	the cars, trucks, etc. using a road
traffic jam	/ˈtræfɪk ˌdʒæm/	(n)	a line of cars, lorries, etc. that are moving slowly or not moving at all
underground	/ˈʌndəɡraʊnd/	(n)	the system of trains that is built under London

VIDEO SCRIPTS

UNIT 1 PEOPLE

Narrator: In this video, and in the course, you meet people from many different countries. You learn about their jobs and their families.

In the United States ...
Amarel works in New York. She is a teacher.
Amarel helps the children with their work and she asks them lots of questions.
The children show Amarel what they are doing.

In Mexico ...
Sebastian is an artist.
Sebastian is famous in Mexico. His art is important.
You can see some very large pieces of Sebastian's art in Mexico City.

In Italy ...
Angela Missoni lives in Milan.
She is a famous fashion designer and she works with her family.
They make beautiful clothes.

In Egypt ...
Yasmine lives in Cairo, where she works for a fashion magazine.
She talks on the phone to journalists every day.
She enjoys her job. Yasmine lives with her mother and grandmother. They help her with the magazine.

In South Africa ...
David lives on the Cape Peninsula.
He is a fisherman.
David catches fish every day and he teaches his sons how to fish.

In India ...
Geeta lives in New Delhi.
She plans weddings. Geeta plans 500 weddings a year. Three hundred people work for Geeta.

The people in this video speak different languages and do different jobs. But they all have one thing in common: they all have interesting lives.

UNIT 2 EXTREME WEATHER

Narrator: The northwest of the United States is an area with tall mountains and thick forests. The air is cold and so there is snow – a lot of snow! – up to about 15 metres a year. And when it is windy, the snow becomes a blizzard. A blizzard is a snowstorm with very strong winds.

In a blizzard, there is snow everywhere – in the cities, in the country and on the roads. A blizzard is very dangerous. Many roads close. When roads are open, drivers can't see. A blizzard can last for three hours and it is very cold. The temperature falls to minus 12 degrees Celsius.

The big, white cloud you can see here is a storm. It is going toward the northwest of the United States. In the cold air of the mountains, the storm becomes a blizzard. Snow begins to fall from the clouds.

Snow can be a big problem for people, like the driver of this car. Near the mountains and forest, there is more and more snow. He has a good car but it becomes stuck in the thick snow. He leaves the car and tries to walk. But it is cold and he is far from the city. He goes back to his car. The car is a safe place for him. There are tomatoes to eat and water to drink. The car is cold but he can turn on the engine to keep warm. Every day, he cleans snow from the car so people can see him. This blizzard lasts for 15 days. Finally, a policeman sees the car. The driver is saved!

UNIT 3 LIFE UNDERGROUND

Narrator: Coober Pedy, South Australia.

It is hot here. The average temperature can get as high as 55 degrees Centigrade. How can people live here?

The answer? They live underground. They make houses from the rock. These houses are comfortable. Dust can be a problem. But the people vacuum every day. Almost 3,000 people live in houses like this one. But why do people live in Coober Pedy?

They live here to work in the opal mines. This is an opal. You can sell a good opal for 50,000 dollars! Ninety-five percent of all opal in the world comes from Australia.

Milena Telak is from Croatia. She is an opal miner. Every day, Milena goes to work in her opal mine. She likes her job. She likes working underground. Milena works with other miners. They use big machines to cut the rock.

What do people in Coober Pedy do in their free time? They play golf! It is too hot to play in the day so they play at night. They use bright green golf balls.

UNIT 4 FRANCE

Narrator: France is in Western Europe. It is famous for its culture, fine food and beautiful countryside.

The French flag is called the Tricolore. It is red, white and blue.

Paris is the capital city of France. Paris is an important city for business and tourism.

This is the Eiffel Tower. It is the most famous place in Paris. Six million tourists visit the tower every year. Another famous place is the Louvre. There are 30,000 works of art in this museum!

Tourists enjoy the fine food. There are 20 different kinds of bread and 350 different kinds of cheese in France. The food comes from the many farms in France.

France is also famous for its mountains, the Alps and Pyrenees. The Tour de France bicycle race happens every year. The cyclists race all over France.

France is an interesting place to visit.

UNIT 5 TAI-CHI AND SHAOLIN KUNG-FU

Narrator: Life is busy in China. The people work hard. Health is important so sports and exercise are popular here. One popular kind of exercise is Tai-chi.

Every morning, about 200 million people in China do Tai-chi. It is popular with women and men. Tai-chi is a good kind of exercise for old people. It is good for the body and for the mind. It is healthy and relaxing. Tai-chi is from China. It is hundreds of years old. Tai-chi is a 'soft' martial art. That means it is slow and calm.

There are also 'hard' martial arts. These men are doing Shaolin Kung-fu. Shaolin Kung-fu is over 1,500 years old. Shaolin Kung-fu is fast and dangerous. You have to be very fit and strong to do 'hard' martial arts.

The man in the brown clothes is Master Li-Yu. He teaches Shaolin Kung-fu to 30 young students. The students practise every day. They work hard. The students are young.

Li-Yu: Kung-fu is difficult. You must practise every move many times.

Narrator: Sports like football and basketball are also popular in China. But martial arts like Tai-chi and Kung-fu are part of Chinese culture and history.

UNIT 6 DABBAWALLAS

Narrator: Mumbai, India. This is a very busy city. The roads are crowded with people and bicycles, cars and animals. Mumbai is an important city. There are many big companies and offices here.

The man on the bicycle is a 'dabbawalla'. A dabbawalla takes food to people in offices.

More than 200,000 workers in Mumbai want home-cooked food. Dabbawallas take food from small kitchens like this and deliver it to businesses and offices in the city. Cooks put the food into a tiffin tin – a special type of lunchbox.

The dabbawallas take the tiffin tins to the train station.

The dabbawallas put the tins in coloured bags or they paint symbols on the tins. The colours and symbols show them where to take each lunch. They put the lunches on the correct trains so they go to the correct person.

The dabbawallas go by train, bicycle and on foot to deliver the lunches. There are about 5,000 dabbawallas in Mumbai. The dabbawallas work very well. There is only one mistake in every 8 million deliveries.

UNIT 7 BUILDING THE NEW SHANGHAI

Narrator: Today, cities are even bigger, busier and more exciting. The buildings are taller, the lights are brighter and there is more traffic.

This is Shanghai. In 1990, around 14 million people lived here. Now, there are more than 23 million! It is important to build more homes here – and fast! These men work at night. They are building apartments.

This is Vincent Lo. He is from Hong Kong. Vincent's company makes buildings in every part of China. Today Vincent is looking at a new project in Shanghai.

Vincent: Over here, we'll have a swimming pool and a leisure centre.

This is the view. Over there is a park and a lake. And here are offices.

Narrator: Vincent's company built Xintiandi. Xintiandi means 'New heaven and earth'. It is a new part of Shanghai.

The man with Vincent is Ben Wood. He is an architect. He works for Vincent's company. People like Vincent and Ben are working all over China to build similar places to live.

UNIT 8 MEXICAN FOOD

Narrator: Mexico is famous for its beautiful beaches and old buildings. The country is between the Gulf of Mexico, the Pacific and the Caribbean Sea. It is a beautiful place.

Mexico has many big cities. The biggest is Mexico City.

Food is very important to the people of Mexico. The first chocolate came from Mexico.

Martha Ortiz lives in Mexico City. She is a chef. Martha is opening a new restaurant. There is lots of work to do. Victor Zapatero is helping Martha with the design of the restaurant.

Martha is going to a market. She needs to buy food for the first night of the restaurant. She finds what she wants.

She enjoys making the food. Martha is making a famous Mexican sauce. It is called *mole*. Martha uses chocolate to make *mole*.

The waiters get the table ready. Everything is ready. Martha can now enjoy the first night of her new restaurant. And her first customers can too. Martha hopes her restaurant will be successful.

UNIT 9 SOUTH AFRICAN WILDLIFE

Narrator: Morning. South Africa. This is a land of diversity.

The savannah is the home of about 300 species of wildlife.

These zebras travel in groups called herds. They only stop to drink water or eat grass.

And these are springboks. They are popular in South Africa. Springboks are fast and tough.

Many tourists come to South Africa from other countries. They come to see the wildlife. Lions and elephants are the most popular animals. But there are many other interesting animals in South Africa.

Here is one of them. The rhino is one of the most powerful animals in the world. This rhino is almost 2,000 kilograms. But he can run at 40 kilometres per hour. It is not the fastest animal in the world. But it can be one of the most dangerous.

South Africa also has a diverse sea life. There are more than 11,000 species of plants and animals in or near South Africa's oceans.

Penguins are perhaps the most unusual animals you can see in South Africa. Four thousand penguins live on Boulders Beach near Cape Town. They are not afraid of people! Penguins are very popular with the tourists in South Africa.

South Africa is a land of diversity.

UNIT 10 TOKYO TRANSPORT

Narrator: Tokyo is one of the biggest cities in the world.

Around 13 million people live here. Every day, millions more come to Tokyo to work. Transport in the city is very busy. How do people get to work? And how do they get around the city?

Tokyo has excellent public and private transport. There are over 50,000 taxis. And over 8 million passengers use the urban rail system every day.

The Shinkansen bullet train is a very fast way to get to Tokyo. The trains travel at up to 300 kilometres per hour. They are very efficient. They are almost never late.

Another popular way to commute to Tokyo is by plane. The flight between Tokyo and Sapporo, in North Japan, is the busiest in the world. More than 10 million passengers take this journey every year.

You can check in with your mobile phone.

A modern and efficient transport system is a very important part of everyday life in Tokyo.

ACKNOWLEDGEMENTS

Author acknowledgements

First of all, I would like to thank my students and colleagues in Al Ain and Abu Dhabi who have inspired this book. Thanks as well to the editors of this book: Nik White, Janet Weller, Barry Tadman and Fran Disken. The biggest thank you goes to my husband, Robert Ryan, for his endless support and encouragement.

Sabina Ostrowska

Publisher's acknowledgements

The publishers are extremely grateful to the following people and their students for reviewing and trialling this course during its development. The course has benefited hugely from your insightful comments, advice and feedback.

Mr M.K. Adjibade, King Saud University, Saudi Arabia; Canan Aktug, Bursa Technical University, Turkey; Olwyn Alexander, Heriot Watt University, UK; Valerie Anisy, Damman University, Saudi Arabia; Anwar Al-Fetlawi, University of Sharjah, UAE; Laila Al-Qadhi, Kuwait University, Kuwait; Tahani Al-Taha, University of Dubai, UAE; Ozlem Atalay, Middle East Technical University, Turkey; Seda Merter Ataygul, Bursa Technical University Turkey; Harika Altug, Bogazici University, Turkey; Kwab Asare, University of Westminster, UK; Erdogan Bada, Cukurova University, Turkey; Cem Balcikanli, Gazi University, Turkey; Gaye Bayri, Anadolu University, Turkey; Meher Ben Lakhdar, Sohar University, Oman; Emma Biss, Girne American University, UK; Dogan Bulut, Meliksah University, Turkey; Sinem Bur, TED University, Turkey; Alison Chisholm, University of Sussex, UK; Dr. Panidnad Chulerk , Rangsit University, Thailand; Sedat Cilingir, Bilgi University, Istanbul, Turkey; Sarah Clark, Nottingham Trent International College, UK; Elaine Cockerham, Higher College of Technology, Muscat, Oman; Asli Derin, Bilgi University, Turkey; Steven Douglass, University of Sunderland, UK; Jacqueline Einer, Sabanci University, Turkey; Basak Erel, Anadolu University, Turkey; Hande Lena Erol, Piri Reis Maritime University, Turkey; Gulseren Eyuboglu, Ozyegin University, Turkey; Muge Gencer, Kemerburgaz University, Turkey; Jeff Gibbons, King Fahed University of Petroleum and Minerals, Saudi Arabia; Maxine Gilway, Bristol University, UK; Dr Christina Gitsaki, HCT, Dubai Men's College, UAE; Sam Fenwick, Sohar University, Oman; Peter Frey, International House, Doha, Qatar; Neil Harris, Swansea University, UK; Vicki Hayden, College of the North Atlantic, Qatar; Joud Jabri-Pickett, United Arab Emirates University, Al Ain, UAE; Aysel Kilic, Anadolu University, Turkey; Ali Kimav, Anadolu University, Turkey; Bahar Kiziltunali, Izmir University of Economics, Turkey; Kamil Koc, Ozel Kasimoglu Coskun Lisesi, Turkey; Ipek Korman-Tezcan, Yeditepe University, Turkey; Philip Lodge, Dubai Men's College, UAE; Iain Mackie, Al Rowdah University, Abu Dhabi, UAE; Katherine Mansfield, University of Westminster, UK; Kassim Mastan, King Saud University, Saudi Arabia; Elspeth McConnell, Newham College, UK; Lauriel Mehdi, American University of Sharjah, UAE; Dorando Mirkin-Dick, Bell International Institute, UK; Dr Sita Musigrungsi, Prince of Songkla University, Hatyai, Thailand; Mark Neville, Al Hosn University, Abu Dhabi, UAE; Shirley Norton, London School of English, UK; James Openshaw, British Study Centres, UK; Hale Ottolini, Mugla Sitki Kocman University, Turkey; David Palmer, University of Dubai, UAE; Michael Pazinas, United Arab Emirates University, UAE; Troy Priest, Zayed University, UAE; Alison Ramage Patterson, Jeddah, Saudi Arabia; Paul Rogers,

Qatar Skills Academy, Qatar; Josh Round, Saint George International, UK; Harika Saglicak, Bogazici University, Turkey; Asli Saracoglu, Isik University, Turkey; Neil Sarkar, Ealing, Hammersmith and West London College, UK; Nancy Shepherd, Bahrain University, Bahrain; Jonathan Smith, Sabanci University, Turkey; Peter Smith, United Arab Emirates University, UAE; Adem Soruc, Fatih University Istanbul, Turkey; Dr Peter Stanfield, HCT, Madinat Zayed & Ruwais Colleges, UAE; Maria Agata Szczerbik, United Arab Emirates University, Al Ain, UAE; Burcu Tezcan-Unal, Bilgi University, Turkey; Dr Nakonthep Tipayasuparat, Rangsit University, Thailand; Scott Thornbury, The New School, New York, USA; Susan Toth, HCT, Dubai Men's Campus, Dubai, UAE; Melin Unal, Ege University, Izmir, Turkey; Aylin Unaldi, Bogaziçi University, Turkey; Colleen Wackrow, Princess Nourah bint Abdulrahman University, Riyadh, Saudi Arabia; Gordon Watts, Study Group, Brighton UK; Po Leng Wendelkin, INTO at University of East Anglia, UK; Halime Yildiz, Bilkent University, Ankara, Turkey; Ferhat Yilmaz, Kahramanmaras Sutcu Imam University, Turkey.

Special thanks to Peter Lucantoni for sharing his expertise, both pedagogical and cultural.

Photo acknowledgements

The authors and publishers acknowledge the following sources of copyright material and are grateful for the permissions granted. While every effort has been made, it has not always been possible to identify the sources of all the material used, or to trace all copyright holders. If any omissions are brought to our notice, we will be happy to include the appropriate acknowledgements on reprinting.

p.12: (1) © Eric Limon/Shutterstock; p.12: (2) © szefai/Shutterstock; p.12: (3) © Steven Vidler/Eurasia Press/Corbis; pp.14/15: © Mitchell Funk/Getty Images; p.19: Allstar Picture Library/Alamy; p.21(T): © Bernd Thissen/epa /Corbis; p.21(B): Burak/Getty Images; p.26(L): Image source/Alamy; p.26(R): © Takayuik/Shutterstock; pp.32/33 © Maurizio Rellini/SOPA/Corbis; p.34(L): Fwwidall/Getty Images; p.34(C): Ocean/Corbis; p.34(R): © Jose Luis Pelaez/Inc; p.37(T): RIA Novosti/Alamy; p.37(B): © Bill Bachman/Getty Images; p.39: © Kamira/Shutterstock; pp.50/51: © Lonely Planet/Getty Images; p.55(T): Auremar/Shutterstock; p.55(R): © Sergey Uryadnikov/Alamy; p.55(L): © Anders Ryman/Alamy; pp.68/69: Momatiuk-Eastcott/Corbis; p.73: Getty Images; p.75: © AFP/Getty Images; p.77(L): Photo Gersen/Shutterstock; p.77(R): Ocean/Corbis; pp.86/87: © Justin Bailie/Aurora Photos/Corbis;p.91(C): © Chris Helgren/Corbis; p.91(B): © Thomas Melzer/Corbis; p.91(T): European Sports Photographic Agency/Alamy; p.93: © Stuart Freedman/Corbis; p.94: © AFP/Getty Images; pp.104/105: © Galen Rowell/Corbis; pp.122/123: Imagine China/Corbis; p.127(TR): Jetta Productions/Getty Images; p.127(TL): Getty Images; p.127(TC); p.127(TC): Deconphotostudio; p.127(CR): ©Lada Hrsnk & Danielle Huis & Thomas Lenden; p.131: Hemis/Superstock; pp.140.141: © Steve Vidler/Corbis; p.145(TL): Marxman Images/Alamy; p.145(BR): © Danita Delimont; p.145(BL): iStock/© Patrick Heagney; p.146(1): © Viktar Malyschchyts/Shutterstock; p.146(2): Lithian/Shutterstock; p.146(3): Monticello/Shutterstock; p.146(4): © Angelo Gilardelli/Shutterstock; p.147(T): Zurijetn/Shutterstock; p.147(C): © Andrew Watson/Alamy; p.147(B): © Tim Hill/Alamy; p.149(1): © Iilya Akinshin/Shutterstock; p.149(2,3,4): iStockphoto/Thinkstock; p.149(5): © Piotr Malczyk;

Corpus
Development of this publication has made use of the Cambridge English Corpus (CEC). The CEC is a multi-billion word computer database of contemporary spoken and written English. It includes British English, American English and other varieties of English. It also includes the Cambridge Learner Corpus, developed in collaboration with Cambridge English Language Assessment.

Illustrations
Illustrations: Rudolf Farkas (Beehive Illustration) p 79; Fiona Gowen p 78; Martin Sanders (Beehive Illustration) pp 42, 77, 178 (map); Simon Tegg pp 39, 52, 129

Picture research by Alison Prior

Typeset by emc design ltd

Dictionary
Cambridge dictionaries are the world's most widely used dictionaries for learners of English. Available at three levels (Cambridge Essential English Dictionary, Cambridge Learner's Dictionary and Cambridge Advanced Learner's Dictionary), they provide easy-to-understand definitions, example sentences, and help in avoiding typical mistakes. The dictionaries are also available online at dictionary. cambridge.org. © Cambridge University Press, reproduced with permission.